AIR

Dean Spears is a visiting researcher at the Economics and Planning Unit of the Indian Statistical Institute in Delhi, an assistant professor at the University of Texas at Austin, and an executive director of r.i.c.e., a research institute for compassionate economics. He is affiliated with the Princeton University Climate Futures Initiative, the Institute for Futures Studies in Stockholm, and the IZA Institute for Labour Economics. With Diane Coffey, he wrote the award-winning book, *Where India Goes: Abandoned Toilets, Stunted Development, and the Costs of Caste* published by HarperCollins India in 2017.

C000161340

Praise for *Where India Goes*

'The best social science book I have read in years'
– Alex Tabarrok, Marginal Revolution

'Combining a data-driven approach and often poignant personal accounts ... a fresh and compelling perspective'
– Abhay Rao, *Stanford Social Innovation Review*

'Deeply researched and thoughtfully written ... reflects on the difficult road of development beyond conference platitudes and technocratic solutions'
– Uma Mahadevan-Dasgupta, *The Hindu*

'"Stunningly well done" and "fascinating" ... dramatic ethnographic case studies and well-documented statistical arguments [of] great potential value to both policymakers and general readers'
– AIIS prize committee

'One of the most admirable and important books I've ever read'
– Rahul Jacob, *Business Standard*

'Essential reading not only for policymakers and development professionals, but for anyone interested in the paradoxes of development in the early 21st century'
– Govindan Nair, The Wire

'Important, timely, and easy to read'
– Sudhirendar Sharma, *Hindustan Times*

'A path-breaking and brilliant addition to the literature on child malnutrition and development policy in India'
– Awinash Kumar, The Wire

AIR

Pollution, Climate Change
and India's Choice Between
Policy and Pretence

DEAN SPEARS

HarperCollins *Publishers* India

First published in India by
HarperCollins *Publishers* in 2019
A-75, Sector 57, Noida, Uttar Pradesh 201301, India
www.harpercollins.co.in
2 4 6 8 10 9 7 5 3 1

P-ISBN: 978-93-5357-082-8
E-ISBN: 978-93-5357-083-5

Typeset in 10.5/13.3 Adobe Caslon Pro at
Manipal Digital Systems, Manipal

Printed and bound at
Replika Press Pvt. Ltd.

to
r.i.c.e.

Contents

List of Figures

Introduction

Across the street from the most distinguished conference halls in Delhi, around the corner from the international offices of UNICEF and the World Bank, a tall electronic board shows numbers about air pollution. Traffic idles at a signal as the display cycles through a list of colour coded details: concentrations of particles of certain sizes, counts of other chemicals. Sometimes, in the winter, the numbers are blank when the pollution is off the scales. But when I started writing this book in June 2018, a quantity called '$PM_{2.5}$' was around 55 and was colour coded green. June is one of Delhi's better months in terms of air pollution. The display signals to citizens and passers-by that the air quality is 'satisfactory'.

It is not. As scientists and regulators around the world agree, so much pollution is hazardous. In the UK, it would be coded red for 'high'; in the US, red for 'unhealthy'. But, for the purposes of this sign and other official claims, the Indian state has adopted its own colour scheme. The green digits are a reassuring message from the government: pollution levels are under control.

At another time of the year, Delhi's colour codes will be in the news: pollution in the summer is low compared to the heights it

1

reaches in winter. The city's air pollution receives more than its fair share of newspaper articles. It also has more pollution monitors than in any other Indian city. Of the 134 Central Pollution Control Board air monitors, thirty-six are in Delhi.

A few years ago, a jumbo screen appeared in Hazratganj, dominating the main intersection of Lucknow. Hazratganj is the poshest part of the Uttar Pradesh (UP) capital. It is a line of shops between the state legislature and the towers that house the state administrative bureaucracy. Throughout Lucknow, there are four air monitors. They record pollution levels not so different from Delhi's.

The state government's signboard in Hazratganj does not colour code air pollution. Unlike the screen in Delhi, the enormous Lucknow display rotates through the achievements of the UP government, rather than counts of particles in the air. Across the intersection, obscured behind another board, Lucknow does have its own sign about pollution: 'Uttar Pradesh Pollution … Present … SO_2 NO_X' is all that is visible behind the advertisement in front. This display is broken. The pollution concentrations are supposed to be shown on a busted display behind cracked glass.

In Kanpur, ninety kilometres from Lucknow, I have never seen any display of pollution counts. Three million people live in this city of Kanpur – a little more than that in Lucknow. Somewhere in Kanpur, there is a machine that measures air pollution. In having one machine at all, Kanpur is lucky: there are only fifteen government air pollution monitors for the 200 million people of Uttar Pradesh. The Brazilian state of São Paulo, home to one-fifth as many people as UP and much less polluted, has eighteen.

Kanpur does have an office of the Uttar Pradesh Pollution Control Board. The office is at the end of a middle-class residential neighbourhood, a little further down from a colourful private preschool. Just past the pollution office, the street turns to grass at a grey nali, where weeds grow bright green and cows graze. Electrical wires from the houses gather to rise above the nali. The confluence of wires lifts my gaze further up to the smokestack, just across the way.

The tower of the Panki coal-fired power plant rises above. The plant is shaped like an asymmetric N: a long ramp moves the coal, the tall smokestack releases the fumes. The Kanpur coal plant is only 400 kilometres from Lodhi Estate, where the sign reports pollution counts at Delhi's elite office blocks.

Covering the problem with a tarp

Ravi owns a cloth shop in a tent near the coal plant. His father came to Panki from Hamirpur in Himachal Pradesh. Since 1980, he has lived within a kilometre or two of the coal plant.

These days, Ravi has the fully-stuffed shirt pocket of a UP businessman. The first day he reached Kanpur, Ravi sold sixty rupees' worth of water chestnuts in the afternoon. Ravi worked his way up to owning a shop, starting from selling tea outside Gate 1 of the coal plant. He remembers when some 'big minister' came to inaugurate two units of the plant. On a hot May day, when customers were not out shopping, he was happy to tell about it.

Ravi accuses the obvious problem: ash. 'The chimney emits ash and smoke, and it flows with the wind. It is a big problem for everyone: everyone on the road, the people who live around the plant, the shopkeepers. The ash goes in people's eyes. Clothes on the clothesline turn ash-coloured. You cannot sleep on the roof at night.'

Ravi's father suffered from asthma. Ravi suspects that he died from it, and that the coal plant gives people heart attacks. Back in the day, Ravi remembers, he could not afford a clean place for his father to sleep. He lived near the coal plant, selling tea outside of Gate 1. Even after he had a shop, he could not afford a separate home, so his family slept there in a tent.

Ravi sat cross-legged under his display of ornate outfits for little girls. When he was selling tea and snacks, the plant was a ready source of customers. At one high point, he was even able to expand and open a shop at Gate 2. Ever since he moved on to selling clothes, though, the coal plant has threatened his merchandise with ash. Trucks take ash from the coal plant. Some of the trucks, over the years, have gone to cement factories to make bricks, Ravi believes. On the way, the ash spills everywhere.

Some of the ash leaves the coal plant through smokestacks, rather than in trucks. When I first learnt about the polluting effects of coal plants, I assumed ash to be the problem. But environmental health can be surprising. The science says there is not a lot of ash in coal emissions.

What coal plants, in fact, release much more of are the chemicals SO_2 and NO_X. These waft downwind of the coal plant to somewhere else. Along the way, chemical reactions in the air turn these pollutants into $PM_{2.5}$: tiny particles which go deep into the smallest air sacs within human lungs, and from there to the bloodstream. Coal plants also produce carbon emissions – the gases that trap heat, causing global warming and climate change.

Such tiny pollutants are only visible in careful studies. But it is easy to get the people who live near the Panki plant to talk about the ash trucks. Agnihotri comes from a privileged Kanpuri family. They own a private school in the nearby semi-urban village. Over the years, land there has been bought by and absorbed into the coal plant. Now, he is the principal of the school, in an office away from the plant. With a desk, chairs and a cooler, it feels far from the mat in Ravi's shop. Over tea, Agnihotri explained that the coal plant gave jobs and economic development to a barren village that needed it. To him, the coal plant brings many benefits, even if (he recalled from a public meeting) it was intended to be shut down three years ago.

Agnihotri had to admit: the coal plant also sends those unfortunate ash trucks. He took pains to emphasize the wisdom of the officials who decided to build and expand the coal plant. Still, the trucks led to 'ash flying around'. So, Agnihotri recalled, the government took the reasonable step of covering the trucks with tarps, that is, with plastic sheets on top.

Ravi remembered those tarps, too. As the trucks rumbled from the coal plant, the tarps flapped and kept some of the ash inside – but not all of it. The tarps did not keep the ash from spilling onto the samosas he hoped to sell.

Ravi and Agnihotri will never sit together and talk about energy policy. If they did, they would have a lot to agree about. Both believe that the coal plant brought business, jobs and property wealth. Both agree that ash is a nuisance and that it makes people sick (they both mentioned asthma). But they disagree about the tarps: Agnihotri is comforted that the 'wise and educated people in the government' have things in hand; Ravi is less impressed.

Why would the government bother to cover the trucks with tarps that do not prevent the ash from spilling out? When I heard about these tarps, I wondered who they are for. Are they for Agnihotri, who reflects on them from a distant office, or for Ravi, who sits along the road, where the ash still falls anyway?

Are these men right about the benefits of the coal plant to the economy? Do these benefits justify the health risks? And are Ravi and Agnihotri correct to stress the obvious problems – ash, coughing and asthma – instead of other, more subtle, ways that air pollution might damage human health, or the entire economy? As they both realized, much of India's air pollution is generated in the process of improving economies and lives. Knowing how to respond requires balancing the good consequences and the bad – and therefore requires understanding how bad air pollution could be.

How bad is it?

'Come now, Dean: you can't really believe it is such a big deal?'

I had heard this objection before from other people. From my south Delhi landlord, convinced that the tree across the street absorbed the threat. From the men spitting paan into the shadow of another Uttar Pradesh coal plant that dominates their village. From my own frustration, as my wife, Diane, prudently reminds me to cage ourselves in tight with the air filters in our bedroom. Years ago, Diane and I both brushed off a famous newspaper reporter who asked us about Delhi's pollution: we wanted his story to be about toilets, which we were writing a book about.

This time, I was chatting while walking into one of the mirrored hotel conference rooms where Delhi's policy observers talk with one another. The doubt came from a distinguished commentator with impeccable quantitative training, someone famous in policy-making circles. 'Really? Even him?' My editor shook his head when I recounted the moment when I finally overruled my reluctance to write this book.

So, if you are one of the dozens who have asked me if the air pollution could really be such a big deal, this book is for you. Readers who already worry about air pollution face another question: what can we expect the Indian state to do about it? And what do we learn from the smoke it blows in the meantime?

India's air pollution is indeed a big deal. One reason that we will see is because air pollution harms children and babies. Children are important. Everybody starts out as a baby. So, the productivity, health and well-being of the whole population depends, in part, on some surprisingly life-long consequences of early-life health. Another reason that air pollution is important is because much of it turns out to be in Uttar Pradesh and Bihar. Disadvantaged people in these states have the misfortune to suffer worse exposure to air pollution. So, in this way, inequality in health deepens inequality in income.

Mostly, air pollution is important simply because exposure to pollution is biologically harmful and quantitatively extreme in its effects across the entire population of contemporary India. Little particles in the air turn out to have awful, destructive consequences for human health. Hundreds of millions of Indians now live smothered by them.

Two problems in the air

This book is about two different problems. Because particle pollution already causes so much harm, it comes first. $PM_{2.5}$ is a statistic that measures exposure to harmful little particles. It counts the concentration of airborne particles less than 2.5μm wide. Particles so small are fine enough to get deep inside a person's lungs. Fine particles – what $PM_{2.5}$ measures – cause illness today and hurt people now. Addressing particle pollution will be difficult, but India's democracy may offer one advantage: particles emitted within India typically cause harm soon after they are emitted. So, today's voters could demand policies to reduce particle pollution.

The other problem, climate change, involves a different type of pollutant. Greenhouse gas emissions are chemicals such as carbon dioxide, which scientists write as CO_2. Carbon emissions today will harm people for centuries to come. Carbon emissions in one place, at one time, cause future global warming all around the world.

Both types of pollution have deadly consequences, but in biologically different ways. Another difference between these two problems is that, although India could enact policies to clear its own air from particle pollution, India cannot stop climate change on its own. This is because even if India eliminated its carbon emissions, emissions from other countries would be enough to warm the world. Rich countries like the US have done most of the CO_2 emitting; South Asians will bear much of the costs. For all of these reasons, particle pollution and climate change are typically understood to be different problems — which, in many ways they are.

And yet – as we will find – these two distinct problems turn out to come together, when we search for policy solutions. This is especially true for India: among populations of the world, future Indians will be especially vulnerable to harm from climate change. They are already vulnerable to particle pollution. In fact, the hazardous effects of particulate pollution give India good economic reasons to rearrange its mix of electricity sources in order to emit fewer particles. Making that rearrangement in a smart way, and then talking about it internationally in a smart way, could be the strategic solution India needs to its climate policy dilemma. In other words, some strategic policies – such as burning less coal – could clear the air in both ways, with one stroke.

Unfortunately, another similarity between these dissimilar types of air pollution is the challenge of governing the air, especially given the realities of the Indian state. Both forms of pollution have the same easy theoretical solution in economics textbooks. But in neither case is this textbook solution being applied. It is not clear if India's governance – with its combination of market failures and government failures, of democracy and bureaucracy, of highly-educated Central Secretaries and village sachivs – is meaningfully managing either type of air pollution. Nor are many voters – whose only option is to choose one party over another – likely to switch away from a party they prefer merely because the other party promises less pollution. Ultimately, air pollution and climate change are both problems that are easy for leaders to pretend to take seriously while in fact not resolving them, and hardly even monitoring them.

You cannot solve what you do not measure

If the Indian state were managing its air pollution challenges, the first step would be carefully and thoroughly measuring them: keeping track of just how much air pollution there is, where and when. But air pollution data is only collected for a few spots in a few cities. Most Indian voters could be forgiven for missing the danger that air pollution poses to them, given that the government is not measuring pollution where they live – and hardly anywhere else. As a result, this is a book, in part, about clever, hardworking researchers doing the best they can to generate basic information about air pollution. Governments in other countries routinely collect such information, as part of their ordinary job. In India, researchers have to scrounge for it.

Josh Apte is an engineering professor at the University of Texas at Austin. I met Josh because I now teach there in spring semesters. Before Josh was a professor, he was a PhD student in need of a dissertation topic. He realized that he could do a little bit to provide the air pollution data that the Indian state was not collecting, if he could build the right machines.

Around the world, air pollution is usually measured by stationary machines stuck outside tall buildings. This approach can work well, but Josh understood that it has two problems for Delhi. The first problem is that understanding exposure to air pollution requires many monitors, spread throughout a city. King's College in London, for example, maintains a pollution website for the public. Data streams in from 100 monitor sites throughout London, a city which is much less polluted than Delhi. In contrast, the Indian government's few monitors only tell about a few localities in Delhi. Josh needed to find a way to reach more of the city.

The second problem that Josh saw is that because air pollution levels can be so high in India, they can also differ widely between neighbourhoods or days. If air pollution levels tend to be low, there is a statistical limit to how much they can vary. But in north India – where high pollution levels can veer from large to huge one street to the next – one monitor could mean little for conditions a block away.

Josh had an idea. If he could not affix many air pollution monitors throughout Delhi, could he do the next best thing: move an air pollution monitor through the city, using a computer to record the pollution levels it finds along the way? Josh figured out how to engineer an auto-rickshaw ('a single Bajaj model RE-4S TSR vehicle', his scientific publication reports) to drive an air pollution monitor of his creation. Of course, Josh used one of the modern CNG autos. He made sure his driver did not smoke.

When the Associated Press wrote about his findings in the news, they published a picture of Josh's tall body curled up, fixated on a computer screen, in the back of his auto with his machines. The auto plied back and forth along a set route for forty days in February and March 2018. The path looks like mine when I am visiting my friends in South Delhi. It starts in Chittaranjan (CR) Park, takes August Kranti Marg to Lodhi Garden, loops around India Gate (if the air pollution is not too bad, you can see the central ministries) and finishes in Connaught Place (CP).

The air pollution levels that Josh found were enormous. My friend Subha lives in CR Park. Josh computed that if Subha took this route to go to a conference at the Habitat Centre and then a coffee meeting in CP (which she probably has), then that short commute would be equivalent to a whole day's worth of exposure in other polluted cities. 'Official air quality monitors tend to be located away from roads, on top of buildings, and that's not where most people spend most of their time,' Josh explained to a reporter.

At 190 µg/m^3, the *average* exposure to PM$_{2.5}$ in Josh's study was nineteen times the World Health Organization's (WHO's) guideline for annual mean exposure (which is ten). Josh took his measurements in February and March, when pollution in Delhi has begun to decline from its annual peak. So, he did not even capture the worst of it.

Ever more of Delhi's elites have apps and eggs and other gadgets to keep track of their own exposure to PM$_{2.5}$. In the absence of adequate official data, the market supply of monitors has risen to meet the growing demand. But as far as I know, Josh still has the only auto dedicated to the project.

In early November of 2018, I was away from Delhi to present demographic research in Sweden about neonatal mortality in India. Josh emailed me and our collaborators to encourage us all to 'stay safe': that morning in Delhi, his research team had measured a PM$_{2.5}$ of 945 µg/m^3 (an engineering professor does not omit units, even in emails). So much particulate pollution is thirty-eight times the WHO guideline for a day's exposure. In the Nobel Prize Museum in Stockholm, I saw Amartya Sen's bicycle, the vial out of which Barry Marshall drank *Helicobacter pylori*, and Angus Deaton's fishing flies. For helping to show us that Delhi's air pollution really is that bad, maybe Josh's auto will someday join them.

It's time to clear the air

When Yosemite National Park in California caught fire in July 2018, CBS Nightly News described the air pollution as 'worse than Beijing'. The American broadcaster's impressions were years out of date. Air pollution in China is much better than it used to be, in part because of Chinese policy efforts. No Chinese city is near the top of the polluted list of cities now. Indian cities are, though.

India's air is not polluted just because it is poor. Figure 1 shows that average particle pollution in India is even worse than in other countries at a similar level of economic development. The figure includes each country where at least 100 million people live. This amounts to more than three-fifths of the world's population. Each country's circle is proportional to the size of its population, so the other large circle is China. There is a downward slope, which means that richer countries tend to have cleaner air.

But India's air is much more polluted than the international trend predicts for its level of economic development. The only two countries that are close to India's particle pollution are Pakistan and Bangladesh, which share air with India. Both of these – as well as Ethiopia and Nigeria, which are the other two poorest countries in the graph – have cleaner air than India. So, Figure 1 rebuts the fiction that pollution is the price of progress. The air is cleaner in richer countries than in India, cleanest in the richest countries, and also cleaner in poorer countries.

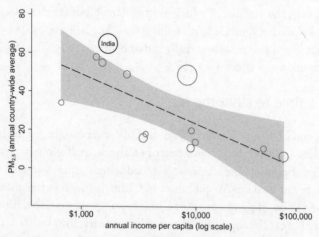

Figure 1. India's particle pollution is worse than other developing countries

In fact, the situation is much worse than what Figure 1 can reveal. India's circle at the top averages over the whole year and the whole country. But some parts of India are much more polluted than others. Remember that Josh found an average of 190 in Delhi in early spring. Delhi and states in the northern plains have particle pollution levels that are much higher than parts of south India. If Uttar Pradesh and Bihar formed their own country, then it would have a population larger than every country besides China, the US, and the rest of India. Its average $PM_{2.5}$ would be well off the top of the chart.

Pollution also varies over the months of the year. November, December and January are the worst. So, in north India in the winter, pollution levels are much higher than sixty-five: commonly above 500, and sometimes above 900. The World Health Organization believes that it is unsafe to breathe particle pollution levels above ten, as a year-long average, or above twenty-five in one day. So, north India's pollution is severe.

In May 2018, the WHO released a list of the most polluted cities worldwide. Kanpur – home to Ravi, Agnihotri, and the Panki coal plant – was number one. The worst. With an average pollution level of 173, Kanpur edged out Faridabad at 172, and came in worse than Varanasi, Patna, Delhi, Lucknow, Muzaffarpur, Gurgaon, Jaipur and Jodhpur. These were worse, in turn, than a city in Kuwait which, ranked at number fifteen, is the first one on the list that is not in India.

I did not know that Kanpur would top this list when, a few years ago, I first started walking around the Panki coal plant. My field research has long orbited around central UP. The two nearby coal plants were in Kanpur and Raebareli. I visited them both, but the Raebareli option became unavailable for follow-up field visits when the coal plant exploded in 2017, killing thirty-two people. I confess I feel a bit embarrassed that so much of this book takes place in 'number one' Kanpur: why visit the *worst* place, when the problem is so widespread?

The truth is that Kanpur is only one point worse than city number two. Kanpur's air is like that of the other Indian cities on the WHO's list, and like the thousands of villages spread between them. Realistically, there are not enough monitors to tell the difference among the top few. Statistically, Kanpur's air pollution fluctuates with Lucknow's, with Delhi's, and with the rest of north India's.

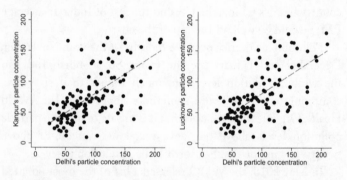

Figure 2. Air pollution varies throughout the year, but is a similarly bad problem for districts throughout the northern plains (each dot is one month's average $PM_{2.5}$)

Figure 2 zooms in on Figure 1, to depict the variation over the year in Delhi's, Lucknow's and Kanpur's air pollution. In Figure 2, each dot plots average particulate pollution over one month between 2010 and 2015. The topmost dot for Kanpur, for example, was November 2013. Notice that the scale in Figure 2 extends to much larger levels of pollution than the international scale in Figure 1. That is because the scale has to include the highly polluted months in highly polluted parts of India. But even the dots in Figure 2 average over a whole month: the worst days, the worst hours, and the worst villages and blocks would be much worse still. Still, the figure shows that average pollution in Kanpur looks a lot like pollution in Delhi and Lucknow. Air pollution does not confine itself to district boundaries.

Finally, Figure 3 zooms in one more time. This graph only includes data from Delhi, and only from two days in December 2018. Air pollution levels in Figure 3 are very high and fluctuate throughout the day. Exposure to air pollution in the graph is far above the WHO's exposure guidelines, plotted in the lines across the bottom of the figure. To understand how high air pollution levels can reach – and how much averages conceal – notice the vertical bars at the right of Figure 3. These measure the full length of the vertical axes from Figures 1 and 2. As high as particle concentrations were in these figures, they reach even higher levels in the detailed data of Figure 3. And it gets worse. Josh's 945 μg/m³ from November 2018 was twice as high as the scale of Figure 3.

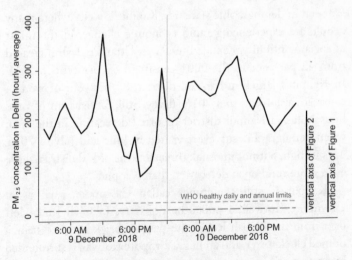

Figure 3. Air pollution varies throughout the day, and reaches high levels in the north Indian winter

The benefits of air pollution

Looking out from the windows of a tower restaurant at the centre of town, Kanpur is a city of smokestacks: brick buildings of red and grey, chimneys above them, and haze. Bricks are ubiquitous in the walls and in the mud below. Now, the old brick chimneys do double duty of supporting mobile towers. From tanneries and brick kilns, from factories active and defunct, and from a large coal plant, chimneys stick up from the surface of Kanpur like trees in a forest.

Many people breathe what comes out of those chimneys. With 3 million people, Kanpur has a larger population than Chicago – the third-largest city in the United States. Kanpur's district, only one of seventy-five in Uttar Pradesh, had a population over 4.5 million in 2011: more people than in about 100 countries represented at the United Nations, including Ireland and New Zealand.

Seen in demographic statistics, Kanpur is a city where many people are experiencing rapid economic change, in the midst of social continuity. Female literacy in Uttar Pradesh increased from 42 per cent in the 2001 census to 59 per cent in 2011. In Kanpur's largely-urbanized district, 82 per cent of women can read, according to a 2016 survey. Still, 62 per cent of rural households in Kanpur district reported defecating in the open when demographic surveyors visited in June and July of 2016. This is high, but not unusual: three-fourths of UP districts have even more rural open defecation than Kanpur.

Kanpur is still sometimes called Cawnpore, such as at Cawnpore Kotwali, a police headquarters in Civil Lines, left over from the British Raj: white-painted brick with red trim, a domed clock tower, and arches. Cawnpore Kotwali is surrounded by small retail gun stores. Blocks away from Cawnpore Kotwali, Z-Square Mall is enormous: four full air-conditioned floors, with none of the empty storefronts seen in its smaller, distant competitor, Ambience Mall in Lucknow. The first shop in the mall sells officially licensed merchandise of the University of California at Los Angeles. At the mall, a large board advertises voltage stabilizers. A few months ago, Kanpur received an airport with three rooms: one for checking in, one for boarding the daily flight, and one for collecting luggage.

Most people in Kanpur will never shop at Z-Square Mall or take a flight. But many of them have experienced the transition to electrification at home within their lifetimes. More people than ever before can now afford a two-wheeler – and the fossil fuels it burns. Unlike prior generations, they will likely not experience famine, in part because of today's mechanized farming.

Many people in Kanpur benefit from the ongoing changes that have immersed the city in air pollution. Of course, the benefits are not evenly distributed. Simple transportation, electrification and food security are basic entitlements for a decent life in 2019. Obviously, people in Kanpur should not have to give up these must-haves, even to prevent air pollution. Do they have to give them up? Or, is air pollution the price we have to pay for an Uttar Pradesh with an infant mortality of sixty-four deaths among every 1,000 babies born, as in 2016, rather than eighty-nine deaths, as in 1999? This trade-off seems like an economic question. But it will turn out that the answer depends on political choices.

Who is in charge here?

Environmentalists have long been famous for believing that the world is going to hell in a handbasket. It seems so from magazine covers and newspaper reports that everyone else now agrees. Yet, the average Indian knows otherwise from first-hand experience. Child survival and electrification are up, poverty and illiteracy are down. These changes represent enormous improvements in well-being. These are only some of the ways that humans worldwide are becoming healthier, smarter, and richer, across the decades and generations.

The British-American economist, Angus Deaton, calls these improvements the 'Great Escape' – an escape from poverty, hunger and premature death. The ongoing Great Escape is the most important fact of the times we live in. When Deaton named the Great Escape, he was thinking of a story of prisoners-of-war escaping from a prison camp. He chose the name to remind readers that each escape from a prison leaves somebody behind. Like a prison break, the Great Escape has created inequality – some populations escaped before others.

Writers who worry about the environmental consequences of economic growth ask whether development is 'sustainable'. Can we accept the air pollution that has come with electrifying Uttar Pradesh? Maybe we can. Deaton's metaphor applies again: every escape also involves some destruction of chiselled-through walls or filed prison bars.

So, there is a dilemma. On the one hand, if India is getting richer, it seems like it could afford to clean up its act. On the other hand, if environmental degradation is the necessary price that humanity has paid to begin pulling down the risk of infant death and the deprivations of poverty, it would seem foolhardy to stop now.

Should the powers that be continue to accept environmental degradation in poor countries as the cost of human development? Much has been written about this debate. All of it appears to assume that there be powers (and that the powers that be are benevolent). Is humanity indeed 'Escaping' because political managers and policy experts have opened some development throttle to full speed ahead?

If every escape from imprisonment entails inequality and a little destruction, every Great Escape also involves great lies

('I need to borrow this rope to use in the prison laundry'). In development policy, the great pretence behind the Escape is that non-profit managers, development professors (alas, I am both), and politicians are in charge of and causing the changes. Certainly, some policy decisions do matter and can do much good or harm. But in places where government institutions are weak, the Great Escape is happening too fast, too globally, and too thoroughly to be the consequence of the diverse things that non-profits and government officials do. If you think that global progress reflects anybody's policy choice, consider the fact that macroeconomists who study the statistics of economic growth readily admit that they cannot explain even most of the differences in *past* growth – let alone predict the future.

One famous example was the Millennium Development Goals. The MDGs, to those in the know, were eight global targets for outcomes such as mortality, hunger and education. The United Nations adopted the MDGs in 2000 with a 2015 deadline. The MDGs dominated development policy conversations and were hailed for their ambition. Thankfully, the poverty-reduction MDG was achieved — five years ahead of schedule, in fact. The world transformed from about half of people in developing countries living in poverty under $1.25 a day in 2000, to 14 per cent in 2015. But statistical evidence suggests that this was happening anyway: extreme poverty was halved merely by existing trends. So, the poverty-reduction MDG happened, but under momentum, not navigation. Nobody is in charge of economic development.

Politicians pretend, but pollution is real

There is a lot of pretending in development policy-making. Some pretence is inevitable. Data on what happens comes slowly and is rarely conclusive. Economists bicker about price indices and poverty lines. Open defecation is obvious when you find it but requires a sincere and careful survey to measure nationwide. Children in India are unambiguously shorter than would be healthy, but there is only a survey to measure height every ten years. And when the data finally emerges, credentialled experts from fancy universities disagree about what it means. So, with facts so scarce, it is easy to start believing your own policy briefs.

Air pollution and climate change are where development rhetoric meets reality. The harms are large and the numbers are worsening. Other trends go in the other direction. Voters vote for improved electrification. Stunting, open defecation, illiteracy – these are all declining. It would be wonderful to speed the change, but if policymakers merely occupy the stage without making things worse, eventually the Great Escape will do the job.

The point is that air quality is *not* getting better. The air is getting worse. So is the climate. Policy makers cannot rehearse the familiar routines of development policy pretence and expect to receive the familiar reward of coincidental improvement. Environment policy requires navigating the ship of state against the current, not with it. So, it will soon become clear whether the navigator has a compass and whether the captain's wheel connects to a rudder.

What is sustainable development?

Development did not end with the Millennium Development Goals in 2015. Neither did goal-setting. The MDGs were replaced with the new and more numerous Sustainable Development Goals (SDGs). 'Sustainable development' is the phrase that has emerged for whatever is special about the intersection of development economics with environmental economics – for the combination of poverty with pollution.

The terminology has caught on. But what does sustainable development mean? What does this intersection highlight? Does it mean – as some of India's leaders have feared – that environmental issues imply that humanity should not do everything it can to fight poverty? That trees are more important than people? At the un.org SDG website, a dramatic drumbeat reveals with a crescendo that 'sustainable development has been defined' – note the wordy UN passive voice – 'as development that meets the needs of the present without compromising the ability of future generations to meet their needs'.

So, is sustainable development just the rule that the meeting of people's basic needs should never decrease over time, from generation to generation? Known as the Brundtland Commission definition, this notion of sustainable development as 'life not getting worse' has become a consensus. But it offers little guidance to the complexity of change in Kanpur. Philosophers have long debated what counts as a need. Sometimes new needs are invented. Sometimes something gets worse, but nobody minds, such as the decline of horsemanship in the mechanizing 20th century.

What stands out about this definition is how *undemanding* it is: as long as the Great Escape continues, as long as we avoid the greatest catastrophes of climate change or resistant infectious disease, living standards are likely to continue merely not to decrease. Surely it matters if things could be even better? Surely we should not settle for the best lives in Uttar Pradesh in the year 2100 being merely not worse than the best lives in Uttar Pradesh today?

Throughout this book, we will reconsider what should be meant by sustainable development. What is special about environmental policy in a developing country? One intersection between pollution and poverty is the new economics of health and human capital. Here, there is no conflict between a clean environment and economic development. The reason is that the newest generation of economics research shows that the health of a population's children in early-life is a crucial determinant of their lifelong productivity. Babies' health and human capital can face lasting harm by exposure to pollution.

The intergenerational transfer of gradual improvements from child to adult mother, to child to adult mother, is one of the paths along which development progresses. Exploiting the economic returns to human capital requires a healthy environment. Unfortunately, however, the poorest populations – who most need a healthy start to escape poverty – also tend to be the ones exposed to the most pollution.

Another overlap between environmental policy and development policy is the recognition that developing countries often have weak governments, or what political scientists call low 'state capacity'. Environmentalists like to publish book-length lists of all the policies and steps that urgently must be adopted to prevent disaster (to be fair, development experts like such lists too). But anybody writing such a list about India must pause and ask: who exactly is going to do these things?

The Indian state has its specialties – rural construction projects, for instance – but it is not an all-purpose institution. It is better at building schools than at getting children to attend them; it is better at administering tests than producing learning. Per capita, India has fewer state employees relative to its population size than other countries. And, beyond the constraints of what the state *could* accomplish, there are the limits on what it *chooses to*: policy is influenced by politics in every country.

India's experience should call environmentalists to realism about developing countries' governance constraints. But just because India's leaders are constrained does not mean they are immobilized. Political choices can build new capacities and activate hidden strengths – or political choices can accept things as they long have been.

What this book is about

I am lucky enough to work with research collaborators who inspire me with their smarts and dedication. You will get to meet some of them, especially those who work with me at r.i.c.e., a research organization that I started with my wife, Diane Coffey. This book talks about my team's research, but few – maybe none – of the underlying ideas in this book are entirely our inventions. Sometimes, we have found ways to use Indian data to demonstrate facts that other researchers already proved in other countries. One goal of this book is to help you see where the science of environmental policy comes from. Many of the challenges are merely in finding or constructing adequate measurements of neglected problems. A consistent lesson is that it is possible to know enough to set principles for policymaking even without answering every scientific question – especially when leaders have made the political decision not to collect data.

Because I can only share the stories of discovery that I know, you will get to know my collaborators. But the people you will meet in this book are a tiny part of the scientific whole. We build on the work of other scholars. Other researchers discovered or computed many of the numbers that you will read. I cite them in the extensive notes at the end of the book. Many readers of this book will know more than I do about some part of it.

Another awkward fact is that, although I have lived and worked in India for many years, I was not born here. Diane and I work together with our friends in India. We call it our home. There is little that is defensible in the current environmental policies of the country where I was born – but I admire that, over the decades, the US has offered a new home to many families born in India. My family made the reverse migration. Still, I did not breathe India's air as a baby. Like some of my Delhi-based economist colleagues who grew up in other parts of India, I learned Hindi as an adult – and my friends still correct me often.

I am an economist and a demographer, so this book is about statistics. I fear that some people will see the opportunity to call me an outsider as a reason to dismiss the statistics in this book. But I have no power over India's environmental policy, or even over whether you read this book. My only option is to invite you to read it. I have some facts, some numbers, and some arguments. Maybe you will find them informative or persuasive.

∾

India's air pollution is not one problem. We have not reached this point merely because one matter was mismanaged. India's air is the result of several governance failures in response to several market failures. Many consequences will unfold, now and in the future. Such complexity is why we need a whole book.

One paradox is about what we know. Although there remains much uncertainty about particle pollution and climate change, we know enough to get started. Unfortunately, much of our ignorance – about air pollution, emissions, health and mortality – is because a succession of governments of both parties have chosen not to observe and record the facts. But some policies – such as shifting electricity generation out of fuels that contribute to both particulate pollution and climate change – are undeniably good ideas, even knowing only what we know.

Still, today's environmental challenges demand a departure from the habits of the Indian state. Ambiguity is threatening, but it also offers a place to hide. If nobody understands the causes and consequences of a problem, it is easier to pretend to address it. Such policy pretence has been common. Maybe, for such an overwhelming problem, this is understandable. But policymakers need not be overwhelmed. They could take those policy steps that are now open and clear, while also investing in the knowledge, data and institutions that soon could do better.

The next three chapters present the evidence that air pollution is already causing important harm. Chapter 1 focuses on health consequences of particulate pollution. Unfortunately, governments on both sides have declined to collect high-quality health data. Statistics about health are almost as absent and inadequate as air pollution data. Most deaths in India are not tabulated into a mortality register, as they are in other countries. Instead, researchers make do with sample surveys.

By chance, one important dimension of child welfare that has recently been measured throughout India is the height of children. The average height of a population is an important number because it summarizes health in the earliest months of life. In a large population, average height predicts the health and productivity of the adult population that children will become.

Exposure to particulate pollution at the beginning of life reduces children's growth. The effect on any one child is not enormous: air pollution is a small part of India's big stunting challenges. Still, a small effect on the height of hundreds of millions of children adds up to a big deal. Moreover, the detectable effect on height is important because it is something that we can see. It points towards an important effect on infant mortality that is concealed by the absence of adequate mortality records.

In Chapter 1, we will also learn the unfortunate truth about how much good a home air purifier can do for you. I told a friend and collaborator in Delhi that I was writing this book. She coughed throughout the conversation, lamenting: 'I thought the pollution problem was all made up by the air purifier companies.

But I was at the doctor yesterday, and my cough is not going away.' Purifier companies did not invent this very real problem, alas. But she is right to be sceptical that purifiers for sale can solve it. Air pollution is a collective, public challenge from which you cannot buy your own private escape.

Chapter 2 moves to rural India. Air pollution does not respect the divide between rural and urban, nor between modern and traditional. It is a problem for everyone. This chapter traces air pollution to one of its roots: burning agricultural leftovers in rural fields. Many farmers do so. Indeed, one of the central difficulties with fixing air pollution is that it comes from so many small sources.

Chapter 1 documents the effects of air pollution on children; Chapter 2 tells us how much that matters. What happens to babies has lasting consequences for everyone: for the whole economy of the next generation. This chapter introduces intergenerational externalities. An externality, in economists' terminology, is the problematic case when the wrong outcome happens because the decision maker is not the person who suffers harmful consequences of a decision. So, *intergenerational externalities* are the problems where neither markets nor governments have effective incentives to meet the needs of future children and later generations.

Some of air pollution's sources are small enough to fit in a kitchen. Chapter 3 turns from cities and farms to inside the home. Traditional stoves produce some of the highest air pollution concentrations to which anyone is exposed. A chulha creates externalities too: everyone's lungs are harmed in villages where more families burn dung and wood, rather than clean-burning fuel. LPG and other clean fuels cost money, but we will see that women's social status can be a more important barrier to fuel switching than the economic cost.

≈

The middle three chapters take a longer view. They ask whether it is time to move beyond the old debate between the environment and economic development. Demand for electricity, the threat of climate change, the hazards of airborne particles: each of these three priorities is real and important. So, policy debates are not advanced by focusing on only one of them.

Modern economies need energy. Electrification transforms the lives of the poor. Chapter 4 asks whether these undeniable facts imply that India cannot afford to care about its environment. Although it makes sense to worry about this trade-off, we will see that many Indians can now afford to invest a little in environmental health. One reason is that India is much richer than it used to be. Indians live as long now as people in 'developed' populations did when environmental debates first emerged. As Chapter 4 will show, many environmentalists misunderstood the economic implications of 20th-century population growth. Similar mistakes could happen again. If so, we would be worried about a conflict between economics and the environment that just does not exist. For example, although India continues to face deep human-development challenges, a range of evidence shows that many of these challenges have more to do with enduring social inequality than with a mere lack of funds.

Chapter 5 turns to the even longer run: climate change. This chapter asks what India's best response may be to the indefensible climate injustice of the developed world. It has been understood for decades that climate change threatens India. Heat and a changing monsoon could mean agricultural failures. Rising sea levels could flood big cities, including metros like Mumbai and Kolkata. New evidence shows that future Indians will be even more vulnerable to climate change than is commonly recognized. One reason is because heat is most harmful to human bodies in combination with high humidity: India, especially during the monsoon, stands out for having both.

Seemingly contradictory facts are true all at once of India's climate vulnerability. Many Indians are poor and still without adequate electricity. Ending their poverty and electrifying their homes throughout the day and night should be priority. But some Indians are rich enough to be responsible for a high level of emissions. Still, nobody can reasonably disagree that it is the rich countries (and not most Indians) that are to blame for most carbon emissions so far. Worst of all, despite India's climate vulnerability, it can do little to save itself: even fully eliminating all of India's future emissions would change the most likely peak future temperature by only a little.

For decades, India has been correct to emphasize in international climate forums that the rich countries are responsible for climate change. The rich countries therefore have a duty to solve the problem and to sacrifice the most. Many in India have been doubtful that these nations will ever fulfil this duty. Anyone who was sceptical of the promise of the 2015 Paris Agreement would not have been refuted by the 2016 election of Donald Trump. But India's being correct has counted for little in motivating global change. Today's Indian policymakers owe it to future Indians to do more than to be correct: they must also find a strategic way to respond successfully.

In Chapter 6, we encounter the hope that India's own health and human development may be the kernel of such a strategy. Sometimes, the same activities that cause carbon emissions also cause particulate pollution. Burning coal is a top culprit on both counts. These facts could create a double opportunity. India could both improve health now and strengthen its pragmatic platform in international climate politics. Such a strategy would require only reducing emissions (especially coal burning) to the level that is *already* in India's overall national interest, considering economics, health and human capital. Whether or not such an option exists, we will see, depends on the quantitative details. Other countries do not have similarly promising double opportunities because they do not have India's combination of particle pollution and climate vulnerability.

Finally, the last two chapters consider the policy response to air pollution and what can be learnt from its inadequacies. In an era that combines environmental misgovernance with electoral demagoguery, it is easy to pit elections versus expertise – to believe that, given our scientifically complicated challenges, the problem is that the voters are either dumb, selfish or worse. The politics of India's air pollution, unfortunately, turn out to be little served by the voters or by the policy elite.

Chapter 7 makes the experts look bad. Experts have an important role in environmental policy because scientific details matter. But just because environmental policy is technical does not imply that technocrats will meet the challenge. Chapter 7 asks why so much environmental policy is misdirection, flimflam, or a theatre of the absurd. It reflects on a question asked by the American philosopher, Hannah Arendt: do governments have to lie when they aspire to make things different, when they hope to change society? Who are the lies for? A reasonable strategy for India might be to project enthusiastic climate cooperation internationally, while levelling in domestic politics with the grim facts of particulate pollution at home. Actual policy has often been the reverse.

Chapter 8 makes voters look bad. It asks whether electoral democracy is likely to solve these problems. Whether to build coal plants, solar plants or metro lines are political questions which could be settled by elections. Nobody, as far as I know, is proposing to give the Indian children born in the year 2100 a vote today, or even a say in these matters that is proportionate to what they have at stake. They cannot take part in our political debates.

Even the voters who are alive to vote now are unlikely to fully understand the problem. Voters do not always make wise decisions. Political scientists around the world have shown that election results respond to random forces outside of politicians' control – like rain. What is good about democracy may not be only – or even mainly – elections, but rather that powerful people are held accountable somehow, to someone.

Resolving the challenges in the air will need accountability and alternative sources of data and information. A democratic civil society could provide that data, but providing public accountability can be a thankless job – or worse. So, Chapter 8 also asks what we can learn from the example of China, which has been tackling its air pollution without the benefits of democracy. India can learn from China's example: what to adopt and what to avoid.

What this book is not about

This book is not an encyclopaedic treatment of every aspect of air pollution or of climate change. For that, consult an encyclopaedia. If I do not touch on a topic (I will not, for example, write about the masks that the publishers included on the cover of the book), it might be because I do not know enough about that topic, so I left it to an expert. While choosing what not to write, I have focused on making space for the evidence that particulate pollution is harmful enough to be important both for today's children and for rethinking tomorrow's climate policy.

You may have noticed that, in summarising the chapters to come, I did not reveal the solution to environmental policy-making. I can tell you now that this book ends in a few big-picture recommendations, followed by many unanswered questions. Oftentimes, it is no big deal if no expert knows exactly what to do. As we learned from the Millennium Development Goal to reduce poverty, sometimes matters work out anyway.

There are many happy stories of improving lives in India. These are the most important stories. Climate change could upend politics through international migration, or could encourage the externalities of infectious disease and antibiotic resistance. But outside of such disasters, the big stories of the Great Escape are likely to continue. So, they do not need a book written about them.

I wrote this book because India's air pollution will not automatically be one of the happy stories. Neither markets nor governments, neither elections nor expertise have all the tools that they need to solve it. The result is that this is a book for several audiences. This book is principally for voters in India, for citizens who care about the health of their society and its human development. But this book is also for environmental policy experts who already agree that air pollution is important but wonder how India will rise to the challenge of whatever sustainable development is. People everywhere are interested in the unknown prospects for a large, emerging-economy democracy to govern the novel challenges of our times. Hopefully, India can do better than the rich countries have.

The 21st century is not the first time that economic development has produced market failures and externalities beyond the state's ability to regulate. But when 19th-century development in Europe and the US caused unchecked harm, it did so with the destructive force only of a 19th-century economy and its technology. It sounds cutesy to say that India is tasked with regulating pollution on a 21st-century scale with a 19th-century regulatory state. But it does not sound wrong when I sit and watch the string-tied paperwork circulate in Uttar Pradesh district offices.

Governments have resolved environmental challenges before. They will again. They had sure better: concerned individuals turning off the light and buying carbon offsets is not going to get us there. But neither the presence of a market failure nor the textbook simplicity of the optimal policy response guarantees that it will happen. The 2015 Paris Agreement on climate change accepted the reality that important environmental policies will be made piece by piece, country by country, through domestic politics and imperfect bureaucracies. If that is going to happen in India, the first step is recognizing that yes, it really is that bad.

Part I
The Short Run

1

Health Outside Hospitals

A concrete boundary wall separates the grounds of the Kanpur district hospital from the surrounding market. Like many borders, it does a better job of announcing separateness than of regulating who or what flows through. When I entered, a dog from the street came along. We both roamed the hallway floors on which patients and their families sat, waited and slept.

Across Mall Road from the hospital, the boundary wall of the central post office bears a government mural. It advertises the national sanitation campaign. That wall, freshly painted, depicts the prime minister sweeping with a broom – a familiar image, except that here his hair is a youthful black. In the painting, his broom waves aimlessly in the air, because no trash or dirt was painted for the prime minister to sweep. The Kanpur hospital has plenty. An open drain flows milkily along the hospital wall, where a pile of trash was heaped chest-high. Some of the trash floated in the drain; some sat in monsoon rain puddles in the hospital courtyard.

Floating or resting along the hospital's inside walls were matches, flies, banana peels, plastic and paper cups and dishes, paan spit, paan wrappers, vomit, human faeces, human faeces

35

in a plastic bag, birds, and six hardened roti, neatly stacked as though for safekeeping. Plastic signs point to padlocked doors with implausible names like 'CT Scan' and 'ICU Ward'. On the ground floor, a level below the ICU Ward sign, I found a man urinating on the interior wall of the hospital. In the several hospital buildings, I did not find a restroom. In the reception hall, a large sign reads: 'We Treat, He Cures'. Below, in smaller letters, a quieter sign requests: 'Keep hospital clean'.

India's health policy debates focus on health treatment: hospitals, doctors and clinics. We Treat. Implicitly, this focus articulates a theory of what health and health policy are: people randomly get sick and the job of the health system is to cure them once they turn up within the clinic. Yet, even within the Kanpur district hospital, infection, the weather and pollution are at work – forces that cause disease and send people to the doctors. Such forces do not usually originate in hospitals, of course. In fact, in India, what happens outside of the clinics may be more important for health policy than what happens within them. Children in India are shorter, on average, than children in sub-Saharan Africa. In poorer countries like Bangladesh, Haiti, and Kenya, a baby is more likely to survive its first days of life than in India.

None of these poorer countries have more money for hospitals or better medical colleges than India does. So, if Indian children have worse outcomes, then much of the explanation must be outside of the clinical system's cement boundary walls. In Kanpur, just beyond the walls of the district hospital is one of the busiest intersections in town. Black emissions erupt from each of the idling buses, attempting to persuade passengers that it is the next to leave for Lucknow. The sound of a car horn is continuous. As crowded as the crossroads can be, there are few women: if the ones who do appear are older than schoolgirls, then they are covered by purdah or ghunghat. And despite the painting of Narendra Modi and his broom, when Kanpur district was visited by a demographic survey in the second half of 2016, 23 per cent of all households and 62 per cent of rural households reported defecating in the open.

Sanitation, traffic accidents, air pollution, the social exclusion of women and mothers: these health hazards add up to millions of infant deaths and tens of millions of stunted children in India. Health policy cannot achieve its goals if it ignores these causes – if it misconstrues its job not to begin until patients cross the hospital's doors. Population health is a scientific discipline that investigates causes such as these. Environmental health or public health are other names for similar research. Population health happens beyond the hospital walls. So, this book does too.

Science outside of laboratory walls

Inside Delhi's research hospitals, medical professors learn from controlled laboratory experiments. Population health scientists do not have it so easy. Undaunted, the researchers in this book work hard to draw the best conclusions they can. They devise the most informative strategies available, with the most reliable data they can find, assemble or measure. Our hero is the 19th century London doctor John Snow, who walked door to door to sort out which cholera cases came from which handpump. In the 21st century, we have engineers who measure air pollution from autorickshaws and from outer space.

India's lack of air pollution monitors is not the only obstacle to studying the health effects of air pollution. Another is that population health scientists do not get to do randomized air pollution experiments. A typical drug trial will recruit a large group of patients with a particular disease. Half of them will be randomly assigned to receive a new drug; the other half gets a similar-seeming placebo. Researchers learn from the difference in outcomes. Of course, few actual randomized experiments turn out to offer perfect evidence. Even so, randomly assigning chemotherapy treatments or childbirth protocols in hospitals is still considered one of the most reliable strategies to link medical causes to effects.

Pollution is not randomly distributed. Disadvantaged children grow up exposed to more pollutants, on average, than privileged children. In the US, poor people breathe one-third more particle pollution than the full population does, on an average. Black people suffer one-and-a-half times as much particle pollution as the average.

In some cases, black children are exposed to more pollution because they are poorer. In some cases, unequal exposure reflects the fact that policy everywhere is more attentive to some people than others. Either way, it is an injustice, and it is not because of the babies' decisions. Poorer people are not merely poorer: they are also more likely to fall ill than richer people (and not only because of exposure to pollution).

Such injustice complicates population science. It is easy to use a statistical dataset to show that people exposed to more pollution are less healthy, on average. But without the simplicity of a randomized experiment, it can be difficult to know what to conclude. Are children who are exposed to more pollution less healthy because of the pollution, or merely because they are poor? The question is as important as it is difficult to answer.

Fortunately, economists – along with demographers and epidemiologists – have been making do without experiments for a long time. After all, inflation rates, unemployment expectations, and technological progress cannot be randomly assigned, even by the most ambitious professor. So, we have econometrics: a set of statistical strategies that we use to learn as much as we can from the variation that exists when circumstances happen to be arranged so that an unusual cause can be linked to its effects. Those cases must be scouted out in the real world. The training of an econometrician is not just mathematical proofs any more. Much of what doctoral students in economics learn is how to recognize one of these special cases and figure out whether it would be useful to learn from.

What traffic teaches

On the bus ride from Lucknow to where I lived in Sitapur, there are two toll booths that collect cash from the passing cars. When luck deals me a bus driver who particularly enjoys his horn, the ride feels longer than two hours. I try to consider reaching the toll booths an encouraging sign of progress.

Near where I went to graduate school, the New Jersey turnpike covers about the same distance. But it has many more entrances, exits, and toll collection points. Despite these tolls, the trip from Trenton to New York takes less time than the trip from Sitapur to Lucknow. The cars in New Jersey drive faster. And unlike in Sitapur, the cars in New Jersey do not stop to pay. An electronic device in the car window, called an E-ZPass, is read by meters which automatically debit the driver's account.

Traffic flowed or crawled along the New Jersey Turnpike long before E-ZPass. E-ZPass was first used for the bridges and tunnels into New York in 1997. In September 2000, the New Jersey Turnpike adopted the invention in all of their toll-collection terminals. E-ZPass spread throughout the region.

Drivers switched to E-ZPass because they no longer had to wait in line to pay: the system read their pass at highway speeds. Janet Currie and Reed Walker, two economists then at Columbia University, saw that E-ZPass might have another benefit. Cars were not waiting to pay, idly pumping out pollution. Because traffic flowed more freely and with less congestion, there was less pollution in the air around the highways.

They realized that E-ZPass could be just the sort of special case that makes a useful econometric strategy. Most children who live near the turnpike are poorer than the average child in New Jersey. But only the children who live near the turnpike and also live near a toll collection booth might have benefited from an improvement in air quality when E-ZPass was introduced. Because E-ZPass spread so quickly and surprisingly, Currie and Walker had a solution to the problem that poorer people live in more polluted places.

Exposure to air pollution mattered for New Jersey infants. Two important measures of health in early life are whether a baby is born prematurely and how much the baby weighs at birth. A baby can be harmed in both ways if its mother is exposed to health threats, including air pollution. Currie and Walker unsurprisingly found that babies who lived near the New Jersey turnpike, but away from one of the toll booths, were just about as likely to be born prematurely and weighed just about as much before and after E-ZPass was introduced. It makes sense that there would be no difference for this control group, because E-ZPass would not have had a large effect on their exposure to pollution. But babies close to the toll plaza weighed more at birth and were less likely to be born early once the electronic toll collection system cleared their air. Because Currie and Walker were only making comparisons among babies who lived somewhere near the turnpike, and because nothing else that matters for infant health is likely to have changed so fast at exactly that time, the impact of E-ZPass offers good evidence that air pollution matters.

Currie and Walker's study joined a long line of environmental health investigations that have found effects of harmful air. Many of these are clever: they manage to find evidence in unlikely places that air pollution is harmful. These researchers do not have the advantage of designing their own bench experiment in the lab. For example, Eva Arceo and her co-authors noticed that meteorological fluctuations in the temperature of the air a kilometre above Mexico City creates unpredictable variation in the concentration of particle pollution in the air near the ground. They used this fact to isolate an effect of particulate matter on infant mortality that could not be caused by another factor. Wolfram Schlenker and Reed Walker figured out that the weather over airports in the eastern US sets off a chain reaction that delays flights in the western states. The delays force airplanes to idle on the tarmac, emitting carbon monoxide. The researchers used this pattern to show that differences across days in carbon monoxide exposure predict hospitalisation rates in California.

Each study devises a different way of escaping the statistical trap: poorer people tend to be exposed to more pollution. Together, the diversity of studies has produced an overwhelming consensus among epidemiologists, demographers and health economists: breathing in air pollution is bad for humans, especially for children. Even in adults, breathing ambient air pollution is known to cause heart attacks, high blood pressure, and lung disease – and to kill people in each of these ways. A 2018 high-profile commission for the medical journal, *Lancet*, reviewed hundreds of studies of the health effects of pollution of many kinds. Two tabulations produced the same estimate: air pollution kills about 6.5 million people each year. Because a total of about 55 million people die each year worldwide, this estimate implies that air pollution causes more than 10 per cent of all deaths.

Staying alive, outside of the district hospital

Our team first met Manju within the walls of a district hospital in Uttar Pradesh. Manju, thirty-three weeks pregnant, had arrived at the hospital the day before in a shared three-wheeler. Her contractions were already well underway when she made it to the upstairs delivery room. Manju believed that she was pregnant with twins. She gave birth to triplet boys. Each weighed about 1,500 grams at birth: the threshold for birth weight low enough that it should be treated as an emergency.

Manju's triplets were not sent to a neonatal intensive care unit: there is not one in the hospital. They were wiped off and handed over to her. The next day, Diane happened to be at the district hospital, as my collaborators at r.i.c.e. often are. She and Nikhil Srivastav had been investigating inexpensive ways to keep newborns alive, such as teaching mothers to hold them right against their warming skin. Over the years, the r.i.c.e. team lived through the deaths of many Uttar Pradeshi babies. Nobody recalls the exact moment that the team decided to draw a line for Manju's triplets, but we did.

Although Nikhil has already written about his work with the triplets in *Outlook* magazine, he and Manju agreed that I should tell the story here too. My own role was small. Nikhil was our leader. He often is, especially in villages. Most of the time, if somebody in this book has shared something important, it is because Nikhil has patiently listened until they wanted to tell it. When Nikhil grew up in Lucknow, it may be that nobody told him how smart he is until he joined the r.i.c.e. team. The result is that his gentle authority is untainted by arrogance: he is at once exceptionally warm and exceptionally competent. Nikhil was just the person to help Manju keep her triplets warm, clean and fed.

Manju brought the triplets home to the village the day after they were born: to a dirt house, with a thatched roof, and a few pots, bricks and plastic jars. According to demographic data, about two-fifths of Indian babies who die in their first year of life die either on the day that they are born or on the next day. So, making it home alive was already an accomplishment. But they were not safe. Outside of the hospital's boundary walls, the threats of population health governed. Manju, Nikhil and the babies' father worked in tireless opposition.

Manju and Nikhil did everything they could to improve the triplets' environment. Diane had a bolt of Superman fabric cut into thirty blanket-diapers, which were always being washed. Manju breastfed constantly. Eventually, when one of the babies would not eat even when fed breastmilk with a spoon, we organized for him to go to a hospital.

And, despite the significance to the family of the ritual, Nikhil persuaded everyone not to light a customary but smoky celebratory fire. Unfortunately, Manju and Nikhil could do nothing about ambient air pollution. The 'door' to the triplets' house was a hole in the mud. Luckily, the triplets were born in mid-March: the beginning of the longest stretch of the year before the fires of the fall harvest and the winter smog. They would have to learn to breathe in the air that Sitapur had.

Learning from India's air

One of Nikhil's worries was that there was little way to know just how much of a threat air pollution posed. E-ZPass, Mexican air inversions, and the weather over North American airports are each inventive and persuasive ways of learning about the effect of air pollution. Finding informative special cases is a useful part of the population health toolkit. The problem with learning from special cases is that they might not answer the question that you need answered: you can only do this sort of research when and where the special opportunities present themselves.

One coping strategy is to apply estimates from one context to another. The *Lancet* Commission produced a report that colour coded each country according to the risk that a person living there would face of dying because of pollution. India was coloured red, in the worst category. The Commission's report cites 418 research articles: it is built on a broad base of scientific evidence that pollution causes death and disease. Still, as somebody who lives in Indian air, I wondered how the *Lancet* Commission knew to put India in particular in that category.

To make such a map, you need to know two things for each country. First, you need to know how high the average exposure to pollution is. Second, you need to know how large the effect of pollution on health is, for somebody unlucky enough to be exposed to it. But there is not one high-quality research study estimating the size of the effect of pollution in each country in the map: most countries do not collect the data that would make this possible. So, maps like this are made by matching country-specific measurements of pollution levels with any available estimates of the consequences of pollution, from wherever such estimates can be produced.

Is it a credible move to use international effect estimates to project consequences of Indian hazards? Ordinarily, I think so: estimates from other places are often good enough to help us think about health policy in India. That is because human biology is not very different across the regions of the world. My favourite example is child height: although different countries' children turn out to have different average heights, the evidence is clear that all populations have the same distribution of genetic *potential* height. Differences only appear because, in countries like India, children are exposed to more disease and malnutrition. But children raised in healthy environments in south Delhi, for example, grow up to be just as tall, on average, as children raised in Europe. Moreover, Indian children adopted to Europe approximate the European distribution of height outcomes. So, if air pollution is terrible for babies in New Jersey, Mexico or China, it is terrible for babies in India too.

∽

There is one way, however, that air pollution might be a little different from nutrition. In the case of air pollution, there may be something important that we cannot learn from most studies in other countries. That is because in India, the pollution numbers are bigger: exposure to air pollution is much worse, on the whole, in India than in other places – even the New Jersey Turnpike. A study from California that persuasively identifies how much worse it is to be exposed to a $PM_{2.5}$ of 20 rather than 10 may not answer the question facing a family in Delhi: how much worse is it to be exposed to a $PM_{2.5}$ of 500, rather than 300? Does every little bit of air pollution count? Or is the damage done at moderate levels of pollution, so that it does not even matter when the pollution gets worse? There is no theoretical reason to be sure of the answer. And there are few other large populations left with enough pollution to find out. So, to answer this question, we will have to use the best data we can find in India.

Josh Apte measured air pollution from autos. Dr Sagnik Dey and his collaborators found another solution to India's failure to adequately monitor its exposure to air pollution: they measured it from space.

Sagnik is an engineering professor at the Indian Institute of Technology (IIT) in Delhi. He is an expert on the technique known as 'remote sensing': using satellites orbiting the earth to measure the air pollution to which people are exposed. Remote sensing is a technique that many scientists have contributed to. It is not as simple as taking a picture of the pollution because the earth's atmosphere is several kilometres thick. Detailed computations are needed to turn the satellite data into reliable estimates of the pollution in the air breathed by people all the way down on the surface. In a series of publications, Sagnik, his co-authors, and other scientists have refined these methods and have proven that they reliably correlate with air pollution measurements taken on the ground.

I first saw Sagnik from the back of an audience: he was presenting his research to an assembly of environmental engineers. Slide after slide plotted equations and tables. I have to confess that parts of it were beyond my training as an economist. One slide, however, was clear even to me: Sagnik mapped computations for each district within India. If remote sensing could separate Kanpur from Lucknow from Sitapur, then we had a chance to learn from differences in exposure to pollution within India. I followed Sagnik upstairs to his next meeting and we made a plan to work together.

Measuring height when data is in short supply

Sagnik's team provided pollution numbers. Working with Sangita Vyas, my long-time collaborator, I matched the pollution data to data on the height of Indian children. Height would be our summary measure of child health.

The height of children may seem like an odd choice for a health outcome to investigate. The *Lancet* Commission was focused on mortality; caring for her triplets, so was Manju. The government has made the absence of mortality data an excuse for policy inaction: in 2017, when he was the Environment Minister, Anil Dave told the Rajya Sabha that 'there are no conclusive data available in the country to establish direct correlationship [*sic*] of death exclusively with air pollution'. Dave's was a poor excuse, because mortality is easier to study in richer countries than in developing countries such as India. The simple reason is that deaths in India are often not recorded.

The most advanced national statistics systems are called vital registration systems: they record all births and deaths. Studies of pollution and mortality use this sort of data. Unfortunately, credible vital registration systems are not found in every country, certainly not in India. As the Monitoring of Vital Events project summarized, 'most people in Africa and Asia, and many in other regions, are born and die without leaving a trace in any legal record or official statistic'.

Mortality is the ultimate summary of health, but until the government devotes more resources to recording deaths, we will need another one. Height turns out to be a surprisingly good second-best summary statistic for the health of a country's children. Comparing one person to another, much of the difference is because of differences in genetic height potentials. But these genetic differences average out when children from all of India are studied together. The differences that are left in population-level data have to be because of health, nutrition, and disease in early-life. So, differences in average height, in a population, are not about genetics.

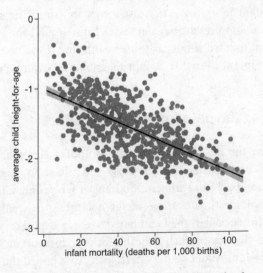

Figure 4. Across India's districts, average child height is closely correlated with infant mortality rates

But why measure height at all? Why not the size of ear lobes, or the width of children's toenails? Figure 4 explains one reason why height is so important. Each dot in Figure 4 is one of India's districts, from a 2015–16 demographic survey. The horizontal axis is the infant mortality rate: dots further to the right are districts where babies are more likely to die in their first year of life. The vertical axis is the average height of children in that district, relative to how tall healthy children of the same sex and age would be.

The clear lesson of Figure 4 is that height and mortality are correlated. Districts where children are more likely to die as babies are districts where the survivors tend not to grow as tall. That is because the children who manage to survive infancy were also exposed to disease, malnutrition, and pollution. Such punishing early-life exposure keeps them from growing to their full height. So, the average child height turns out to be correlated with infant mortality – not just across Indian districts, but in historical and present-day databases from around the world. If you want to learn about early-life health, and if you do not have data on infant mortality, height measurements can be the next best tool.

Tracking the path from cause to effect

To learn the health consequences of India's air pollution, we needed data that lets us link cause and effect. So, Sagnik and a collaborating PhD student, Sourangsu Chowdhury, provided air pollution estimates from satellite pictures: that would be the cause. In particular, they computed average exposure to $PM_{2.5}$ in each district in each month, such as Sitapur in October 2011. Height would be the effect. Josh Apte joined the team to contribute his expertise on air pollution. We were ready to see if the dots connected cause with effect.

The first part was easy: the dots did connect. Children born in district–month combinations where airborne particulate matter concentrations were high (such as Kanpur in Decembers) turn out to be shorter, on average, than children born in district–month combinations where particulate matter combinations are low (such as South Goa in Augusts). The hard part is understanding *why* the dots connect. Is it because of an effect of air pollution on the children, or on their mothers during pregnancy? Or is it merely a misleading coincidence?

There are at least two reasons to worry that children exposed to more air pollution could be less healthy without the pollution itself being to blame: place and time. Place matters because health differs across India's districts for many reasons: women's status, sanitation, and patterns of social inequality vary across India, just to name a few. In other words, different families in different parts of India predictably have different health outcomes. Because these factors are correlated with differences across districts in average exposure to pollution, a simple association between pollution and child outcomes could be misleading.

This statistical challenge is one more consequence of the fact that inequalities often come with other inequalities. Among the 20 per cent of children exposed to the most air pollution in their month of birth, the majority live in Uttar Pradesh or Bihar. Among the 20 per cent born into the cleanest air, only 9 per cent live in UP or Bihar. Studying disadvantage in India is no randomized lab experiment. Our research team needed a plan that could handle predictable pollution.

The other challenge was time, which matters because the seasons of the year matter. In India, air pollution is at its worst in the winter and at its lowest during the monsoon. But this annual cycle could be correlated with child health for other reasons, such as the agricultural calendar or the weather. We had to make sure that children born in polluted months did not appear shorter merely because they had the bad luck to be born during winter.

Fortunately, our survey data gave us just the tools we needed to respond to these worries. One tool is that the survey collected many facts about each child and their family. We could use these to make sure that when we compared two children, we were matching as much as we could about them, except for their exposure to air pollution. In particular, the survey measured children's mothers' heights. A mother's height is important because it is one of the clearest predictors of a child's height. It also reflects the socioeconomic status and environment of the family that the child was born into. Disadvantaged girls unfortunately tend to grow up to be shorter mothers. As a result, mothers' heights, when they are adults, are a useful summary of economic and social advantage or disadvantage.

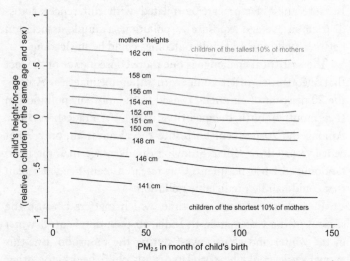

Figure 5. Children who were exposed to more air pollution in their month and district of birth grow shorter, on average, no matter how tall or short their mothers are.

Our data reported the height of over two lakh Indian children. Because we had so many measurements, there would still be plenty in each group if we broke them into ten groups of 20,000, matched according to their mothers' heights. In other words, the first group would be the 10 per cent of children with the tallest mothers: among these approximately 20,000 children, the average child has a mother who is 162 cm tall. The next group is the next 10 per cent, who have a mother that is 158 cm tall on average. This continues for ten groups, until the 10 per cent of children with the shortest mothers, at an average of 141 cm. If the overall correlation between exposure to air pollution and child height merely reflected other types of inequality, we would expect matching mothers to explain away the correlation.

Figure 5 shows that early-life exposure to pollution still predicts child height, even when matching mothers. The ten lines are the ten groups of children: the number in the middle of each group is the average height of their mothers in centimetres. The horizontal axis plots the $PM_{2.5}$ that a child was exposed to in its district and month of birth. Even though $PM_{2.5}$ in the winter can rise to 500 or 600, the graph stops at 150 because it averages over the whole month, including the times of day when pollution levels tend to be low.

The vertical axis is the child's height-for-age, an age-adjusted measure of how tall a child is. A child at zero would be just as tall as the average Indian child of her age and sex. Each of the ten lines slopes down with about the same downwards gradient. So, the correlation between air pollution and child outcomes is not just because of differences in children's backgrounds.

Our other worry was seasonality. Typically, air pollution is worse in the winter. Could the correlation merely reflect some coincidental reason that babies born in the winter tend to do worse?

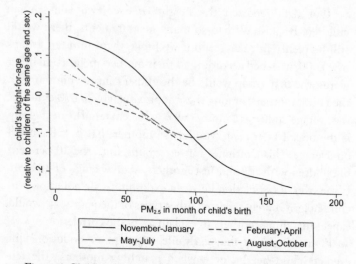

Figure 6. Children who were exposed to more air pollution in their month and district of birth grow shorter, on average, no matter the time of year when they were born.

Figure 6 rules out that seasonality misleads our conclusions. It uses the same strategy that Figure 5 used for handling differences in family backgrounds: splitting the dataset. Just like in Figure 5, the horizontal axis in Figure 6 is air pollution in the district and month of birth; the vertical axis is height relative to children of the same age and sex. The children are split into four seasonal groups, depending on their month of birth. Unsurprisingly, the curve for winter births (meaning, children born in November, December, or January) stretches the farthest to the right: pollution levels tend to get higher in the winter. But all four lines have similar downward slopes. This means that, no matter what season of the year a baby is born in, it is likely to be shorter in height if it is exposed to more pollution.

It is important to start with simple graphs like Figure 5 and Figure 6 before jumping into a complex econometric computation. Otherwise, we might not understand why we find whatever numerical answer our software returns. But once we had seen these graphs, we were ready to program a computer to estimate the effect of air pollution on the height of Indian children. The last step was to settle on exactly how we would handle the predictable rhythm of the seasons. Figure 6 split the sample by month of birth, but it pooled every November birth together across India, and pooled every February birth together, and so on. Seasonal patterns differ across places: the difference between summer and winter in Lucknow is not the same as the difference between summer and winter in Mussoorie or in Chennai. Once again, a solution was possible because we had measurements on so very many children that we could match them precisely, even by their month and place of birth.

The result was clear evidence that air pollution matters for child outcomes in India. We found that children born in months when and where $PM_{2.5}$ is larger by about 100 are shorter, on average, by about 0.05 height-for-age standard deviations. A height-for-age difference of 0.05 is about one-sixth of the average difference between rural and urban children in India. So, on any one child, this is a modest effect. A difference in $PM_{2.5}$ of 100, in contrast, is not small. It is about the difference between what the average child born in Uttar Pradesh in April is exposed to versus what the average child born there in November experiences. But this moderately-large effect that we documented is the average effect for all births in India: it impacts tens of millions of babies born each year. Moreover, air pollution is worsening – although open defecation, for example, has a much larger impact on child height in India than air pollution does, open defecation is declining while air pollution is getting worse.

These consequences add up. In 2012, 26 million children were born in India. Our findings imply that at least 1 million fewer of these children would have gone on to become stunted in the absence of particulate air pollution. Fewer, too, would have died. And almost all of the survivors would have grown and developed towards lives that would have been a little healthier.

Blue skies bluer?: The shape of the curve

Our study was not among the first hundred to document the effects of air pollution on health. Professors always think the world needs another research paper. In our case, we had a particular question that existing research could not fully answer. Studies of the effects of air pollution at North American levels simply might not speak to the effect at India's much higher exposure to air pollution. Pollution going from a $PM_{2.5}$ of 200 to 300 is obviously not an improvement. But is it the same harm as a change from 50 to 150? Or is it not as bad because the damage is already done? Or is it worse? To answer these questions we needed our big sample of *Indian* data, in particular.

Epidemiologists write about a 'concentration-response curve'. The concentration is the level of air pollution. The response is the health impact. And the curve is exactly what we are interested in: how does the health impact depend upon the amount of air pollution? More pollution is never better. But as pollution levels increase, does the extra damage taper off or intensify? What is the shape of the concentration-response curve?

The shape of the curve matters: it partially determines who, among the many people exposed to pollution, should get policymakers' attention. That is because good policy allocates its efforts where they can do the most good.

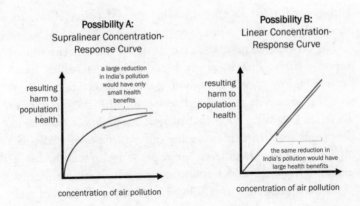

Figure 7. Two possible shapes for the concentration-response curve

Figure 7 plots two possibilities. Panel A on the left gives one example: if the curve is steep at low levels and then flattens out, then it would have the startling implication that nobody would be made much healthier even by a policy that manages to reduce Delhi's winter air pollution by a third. A group of economists led by C. Arden Pope III and Maureen Cropper noticed this possibility: if the concentration-response curve is steep at low levels of pollution (like in rich countries) and flattens out at high levels (like in India) then policymakers would do the most good, all else equal, by concentrating their attention on lower-pollution areas, which are usually home to better-off populations. As Josh Apte, Julian Marshall, and their co-authors once put it, the perverse implication would be that policy should focus on making 'blue skies bluer'.

Epidemiologists would call such a concentration-response curve 'supralinear' because if you plotted the damage at each pollution concentration, the curve would go above a straight line. If we live in a world where the curve is supralinear, then India faces a demanding policy challenge: preventing serious health damages will need successful, multi-pronged policy efforts to bring pollution all the way to very low levels.

Nobody really knows the exact shape of the concentration-response curve. That is largely because the best studies have focused on lower levels of pollution: the high-quality data that such a study needs is from the less-polluted, richer countries. There are scientific papers that suggest a supralinear shape, but they come from stitching together different types of studies of different processes in different contexts: at the low end, ambient pollution from cars in rich countries; at the high end, the effects of cigarette smoking or traditional rural stoves. Even a careful combination of this type runs the risk of a misleading mismatch that combines different types of problems.

Another possible shape is that the concentration-response curve is basically a straight line. That is Panel B, on the right of Figure 7. That is the shape we found in the Indian data: moving from a concentration of ten to sixty is bad; moving from a concentration of 300 to 350 is bad; and none of the evidence that we find rules out the possibility that the extra harm caused by these two intensifications of air pollution would be similarly bad.

Flip back to Figure 5 on page 50: those are lines. Three different types of statistical tests for a curved relationship (instead of a straight one) all suggested that – at least for child height in India – the concentration-response *curve* is a concentration-response *line*. If so, then grey skies matter.

We were able to find this because we had a single large database of children exposed to low, medium, and high levels of pollution. But even though our findings reflect 2,00,000 children, representative of India, they are not the answer to *every* question about air pollution. They are *an* answer. We researchers are tempted to present our results as timeless truths. But the fact of the matter for the height of Indian children now may be different from other countries, from what it will be in the future, or from the effects on outcomes other than height.

One way or another, as long as the concentration-response curve is not completely flat at India's levels of exposure, this evidence is a call to action for policymakers. Reducing pollution concentrations will make children healthier. The largest benefits will come from the greatest reductions – hopefully all the way down to zero someday. But there is a long way to go. Each reduction of the winter peak, from 500, to 400, to 300, and lower, will give children a healthier start to life.

Heal thyself?

If this is your first exposure to the grim statistics of air pollution and health, you may be wondering what you can do or buy to protect your family. So does the government: in March 2018, Reuters reported that 'as pollution choked India's capital New Delhi in recent years, a total of 140 air purifiers were purchased for Prime Minister Narendra Modi's offices and at least six other government agencies'. Once we started learning about air pollution, we wondered the same thing. The filters that took over my family started when Diane found an internet video from China.

Fall of 2014 was becoming winter. Having wrapped up our rural sanitation survey, we were staying in an apartment in south Delhi while we were figuring out what to write about it. Nikhil had not yet met Manju. Like our friends, we managed to ignore the greying of the air. Each morning, I set out to breathe it all in, jogging past a club of deep-breathing retirees, practising laughing in unison. Yet, our team never quite felt completely healthy. Cold, after stuffy nose, after cold wore away my runner's boldness. Sangita, not yet thirty years old and most likely to show up for work still dressed for some athletic exertion, got pneumonia.

The video Diane found online offered a solution and – even more compellingly for her – it included data. While investigating something else in China, a psychology researcher named Thomas Talhelm had worked out a simple alternative to expensive commercial air filters. Most people, even middle-class families in countries like India and China, cannot afford the Rs 15,000 electronic filters for sale in upscale shopping malls. About a year before Diane was googling air quality, Thomas recognized that the important mechanism for any filter to do its job is that air passes through a flat rectangle called a HEPA filter. To force the air through the HEPA filter, a fan pushes the air, leaving the pollutants behind in the mesh of the filter. Everything else – the hypoallergenic plastic box, the blinking lights – is just packaging and marketing.

Thomas's innovation focused on what counted. He strapped an otherwise naked HEPA filter to the front of an ordinary desktop fan. The result looked like a low-budget school science project. In a sense, it was. Because Thomas (now Dr Talhelm) is as data-driven as Diane is, and because he wanted to be right about his own air supply, he switched on his fan and started taking air quality measurements.

The data showed that the homemade filter system absorbed particles. So, Thomas started SmartAir, an organization that would let him market his solution while spreading the word in China about the dangers of air pollution. The video Diane found was by SmartAir and had accompanying charts and tables. Soon she and Thomas were exchanging emails. A box of air filters was dispatched from Beijing to Delhi.

∾

Months passed. Eventually Diane decided that the box of filters might be waiting for her at customs. So, Diane and Nikhil found their way to the right godown at the central post office. Confusion continued – Nikhil explained to Diane on the way home that the clerk had been waiting for the bribe that Diane inadvertently promised – but the visit at least seemed to shake the box loose from the system. A few days later, a large box arrived at the apartment that we were sharing with our team. Labelled 'Diane Coffey' and something else in Chinese, it bore the scars of multiple official inspections for contraband. But it contained only a large stack of HEPA filters and a pile of Velcro straps.

The next winter, the filters went everywhere we slept. Jogging in the park was out; indoor yoga by the roar of the air filter was in. Security guards at small airports throughout the county struggled unsuccessfully to give us reasons why we should not be allowed to have a desk fan in our carry-on luggage. Everybody on our research team was issued a filter and instructions to keep the door closed at all times. One of my colleagues duct-taped a filter into her living room.

Because the fan blows air immediately into the wall of the filter, it sounds like a jet engine with a respiratory infection. Locking yourselves in with one or four of these is not good for family harmony. We wondered: was our obsession with closed doors and bellowing fans getting us anything?

For over a year we had all been walking around with Dylos air particle counter machines. Literally black boxes, they feature a single switch, a small display in 1980s green, and a multi-pin serial port for downloading data, presumably eventually onto a five-inch floppy diskette. Appearances notwithstanding, our Dylos machines could take a beating: we staged a cross-validation after one of them was dropped on the floor. I suspect that they are mainly purchased by the managers of industrial concerns hoping to prevent lawsuits from factory workers by recording federally-permissible labour conditions. The back of the box is labelled with thresholds ('hazardously unhealthy') that, ominously, our air rarely met.

Reassuringly, when you hold a Dylos right up to the do-it-yourself filter, the glowing particle count falls almost to zero. But holding our faces right up to the filter was no way to get our work done. What happens in the rest of the room? Even with a complete set of the black boxes and a matching set of graduate-trained statisticians staring constantly at the flickering green numbers, the risk remained that we were only seeing the benefit of the filters that we wanted to see. So, Sangita started wondering what we would learn from a careful randomized, controlled experiment.

Open minds and closed doors

I met Sangita at Princeton's postgraduate policy school, known for its math and for perpetuating the idea that policymaking is (or should be) based on quantitative analysis. A friend of mine who teaches one of the mathiest classes on the curriculum remembered her, years later, as the top of the class – which, officially, she was. Nevertheless, she forsook career advancement upon graduating from Princeton to join what might reasonably have been described as a policy research start-up if it had an office. When the two of us were the only employees of our new organization called r.i.c.e., each of us stubbornly refused to buy new laptops for our pirated statistical software.

Sangita often has a Stata project or three, whose numbers she can barely wait to crunch, but waits just the same because she finds a higher, urgent priority: getting to a village and figuring out what is going on with some programme or the other before the moment passes, making a survey happen, delivering a TED talk. (Sangita was the first person to read this book, and wants me to clarify that it was merely a TEDx talk.) When she does finally make the graph or table, it usually tells us something important – or, if the numbers do not make sense, she figures out why.

By this time, SmartAir was making its formal entrance to India. Academia does not always reward useful innovation, but in a welcome exception, Thomas had become an Assistant Professor of Behavioural Science at the University of Chicago's business school. Sangita had met, and would soon be marrying, Jay. While the rest of us sat mesmerized by the scrolling particle numbers, Jay saw an opportunity to raise awareness about air pollution. He signed on to help lead the expansion of SmartAir into India. He hit the road with a presentation about the importance of particulate matter and SmartAir's simple, affordable design. Tweets followed. Supply could barely keep up with demand. But Sangita still wanted the facts.

We knew from the Dylos that the filters took particles out of the air. We also knew, from the vast library of existing scientific studies, that breathing particles mattered for our health. What we did not know was the overall effect of the filters on the average particle concentration, in a real-life Delhi room.

We were lucky enough to be sharing an apartment in one of the poshest neighbourhoods of Delhi. But filtering the air will not make you any healthier if the pollution just gets back in. The seal needed to keep out tiny particles is asking a lot of Delhi's construction standards. Our apartment had air conditioning, hot water, drinking water filtration, fancy tile floors, and every other comfort of the upper-middle class. But the doors did not quite fit in the warped wooden door frames; a balcony for laundry connected directly to each room; the windows did not exactly close all the way; and here and there would be a dusty external vent or unexplained old hole covered with plywood.

In other words, a perfectly normal south Delhi flat, on the upmarket end.

Sangita constructed what statisticians call a randomized, crossover, block-experimental design. That means it had a lot of parts. She studied two types of filters: our version of Thomas's do-it-yourself kit and a store-bought commercial filter that cost around Rs 15,000. Sangita tested either just one simple filter, two simple filters working together, or the costly filter. These three conditions were each tried under two circumstances. Under one arrangement, the doors were kept closed. Under the other condition, a 'normal use' scenario, the door to the hallway was opened and closed every half-hour.

A test run lasted three hours. Nikhil and Sangita did seventy-two of these. The tests were sequenced so that each combination would be tested at each time of day and, especially by Nikhil, of night. Between tests, around the clock, Sangita and Nikhil opened all the doors and turned on all the fans, to flush the outside air back into our apartment. At the end of all this opening and closing, Sangita had seventy-two coloured lines of data. Each tracked how particle counts in the air progressed over time as the minutes of the tests ticked on.

The rainbow squiggles plotted good news and bad news. The good news was that the lines sloped down: as time went on, the filters pulled the pollution out of the air. Two simple filters made the particle count decline more quickly than one filter could. The expensive filter even worked more quickly.

The bad news was that the particle counts never got very low. In many cases, even after the filters had been running for hours with the door closed, the particle count was higher than in cities that are considered polluted elsewhere in the world. During some tests, Sangita and Nikhil systematically opened the interior door to the hallway, but they never opened the outside door during a test. Still, particle counts in the test room with the filters running were correlated with particle counts measured minute-by-minute outside of the apartment. This is the worst news: it means that the filters were not enough to keep outdoor air pollution from influencing indoor conditions.

Air filters helped, but not enough. Sangita concluded as much when she published a scientific paper about our apartment. 'The findings of this study indicate that although the most affordable air purifiers currently available are associated with significant improvements in the indoor environment, they are not a replacement for public action in regions like Delhi. Although private solutions may serve as a stopgap, reducing ambient air pollution must be a public health and policy priority in any region where air pollution is as high as Delhi's during the winter.'

Air for sale

We have lived in UP long enough. So much so, that when I tell Diane I am feeling bad, she asks, 'Have you eaten medicine?' That is the polite response to apparent illness: *dava khaya*? It does not seem to matter which medicine. The question makes sense because pills are so easy to come by. India's health outcomes are alarming, but it is not because there are not pills to be had at a few rupees apiece.

I often attend conferences in Delhi about health policy. There, I have heard presenters discuss the fact that doctors and nurses at public hospitals sometimes do not turn up for work. Or, that richer pregnant women are steered towards C-section wards so doctors can charge for them. Or, that a British research team has devised the optimal mix of chemicals for cleaning the district hospital floor. The health policy conversation is about hospitals and clinics. But I have never heard anybody planning how to get all of those pills to all of those shops in village windows. The pills arrive by the work of supply and demand.

The pills appear in the villages because people are willing to pay for them. It is easy to open another window shop from which to retail pills, so market competition keeps the prices low. With a capable state, there would be good reasons to regulate the market for pills in the villages around Kanpur. One reason is that if one shopkeeper sells more antibiotics than is needed, the overuse will decrease the medicine's potency for everybody else. Germs would have the opportunity to evolve resistance to the drug.

Another good reason for regulation is that doctors know much more than their customers do about how much good the pills can do. Medicine was one of the first examples that economic theorists found of a market distorted by asymmetric information. Despite these important caveats, most people in India get their pills from private shops, not from the government.

The market is a powerful tool for selling people things that they want to buy, without any bureaucrat needed to plan the details. No allocation authority in the Sitapur Vikas Bhawan had to tell my friend, Mr Sharma, to keep pills for sale in his shop – across the path from the cold drinks stand in Lal Kurti and the mobile phone recharge vendor. He might not have known as much as people believed he did about whose maladies needed what treatment. It might have been better, all things considered, if not so many of the pills mixed in a marketing kick of caffeine – although who am I to say. The point is that people wanted pills and got them. A big part of the continuing Great Escape from premature mortality has been the availability of antibiotics everywhere. Sharmaji helped make that happen – because hundreds of people in Uttar Pradesh paid him to do so.

∽

The economics of air pollution is different from the economics of pills. Sangita's and Nikhil's experiment taught us as much. Private market transactions can supply a family or an office with air filters. I am among the customers. But even nice houses in Delhi do not seal the air out well enough to be completely effective. In the triplets' house in rural Sitapur there was no hope of separating the outside air from that inside. Moreover, nobody is always at home. Many people in India work outside. Most may as well live outside for all the protection their houses give them from the chemical composition of the atmosphere. Demographic statistics classify a baby as 'born alive' if it ever takes a breath. Many babies' first breath is exposed to polluted outside air.

Clean air is not a consumer good. Filters help, but the private market for filters is no substitute for India coming together to clean up the air collectively. Air pollution is routinely given as an example of market failure in every introductory economics course. Economists also have a simple solution: tax polluting activities, so that polluters have to consider the environmental consequences when deciding how much to pollute.

In a poll of leading economics professors conducted by the University of Chicago, almost all of them agreed that a pollution tax would be a good idea to correct this sort of market failure. Christopher Udry, then a professor at Yale, added a comment to his vote: 'This is about as clear as economics gets.' Yet, on op-ed pages and in this book, we meet officials and economists who argue that economics is the enemy of the environment. According to this view, preventing unhealthy air pollution would be nice to have, but a poor developing country simply cannot afford it.

Contrasting economic efficiency with the environment gets basic economics wrong. Air pollution is what economists call an 'externality': the harm happens to somebody other than the decision maker. The market cannot regulate air pollution because the incentives are wrong: a polluter harms everybody else, and nobody can pay to keep the air they breathe clean. Public collaboration – such as by implementing a tax on polluting activity – is the only way to get to the economically efficient outcome. Getting there would make society better off overall, whether it has a rich economy or an emerging one.

Where does health policy begin?

This is where the economics textbooks stop: air pollution is an externality, so policy should correct the inefficient market failure with an efficient, offsetting tax. If it were that easy in practice, this could be a short book.

One reason that it is not so easy is because, as clear as economic theory is, protecting the population from air pollution's bodily and economic harm does not feel like the government's job. Pollution does not seem like something that somebody *does*; it feels like something that just *happens* each winter. Few voters recognize air pollution as a policy priority. Overturning this misconception may be as important as correcting the beliefs that air pollution is harmless, or that economic theory is on the polluters' side.

We have the tools we need, because the science and economics of population health often overturns misconceptions. We have already seen that health policy is not just about what happens in the hospitals. Nor is it just about supplying pills, in part because the market already does that. But the market cannot solve air pollution. It is an open question whether the government will seriously take up this health policy challenge – and whether the voters will ask them to.

If the boundary wall around the district hospital does not keep anything out, who is it built for? One clue is that it was built by the government. The post office across the street has one, as does every government school that I have seen. Perhaps the walls are built *for* the government: to separate the outside pollutants from the medicines inside, which the government considers its job. Inside the walls is the health ministry's business.

The wall claims that we can separate health policy from population health. *Do We Care? India's Health System* is a three-inch-thick book by K Sujatha Rao, a former union health secretary. The book details India's efforts to provide healthcare at birth to mothers and children. Hospital walls appear here too. This long story includes space to regret a publicly supported non-profit clinic's 'peeling walls and broken windows'. The words *pollution*, *smoke*, and $PM_{2.5}$ do not appear.

My point is not to criticize Rao's book. There is nothing wrong with making sure that clinic buildings and walls are in good shape. Nor does air pollution need to be supervised by the health secretary in particular – although it certainly matters to her job. The point is that only public action can address the threat of particle pollution, which will only happen if air pollution is recognized as a public health problem.

Even such an important step would only be a beginning. The next challenge is that nobody is completely sure where all the pollution is coming from because policymakers have not invested in monitoring pollution. But we should not overstate this problem – we know enough to act on many of the important sources. In the next chapters, we will investigate some of the most important: rural agriculture in Chapter 2, kitchen stoves in Chapter 3, electricity generation in Chapter 4, and especially burning coal in Chapter 6. Journalistic accounts of India's air pollution imply that it stops at the borders of the metropolises, but our search for sources will take us out of the cities. We will find much of the harm caused by air pollution there too. Most lungs in India are in villages.

2

Fields and Villages

Sheher ki dava, gaon ki hava. 'The city has its pills, the village its air.' Sangita heard the saying again and again when she asked village families in Uttar Pradesh about air pollution. She had brought her Dylos to count airborne particles in rural Sitapur in January of 2017. January is about the peak of the annual pollution cycle, but even so, nobody seemed to share Sangita's view that it might be a problem. Village air is how we stay healthy, they meant: the wholesome air is the reason why we do not need medicine.

Villagers are not the only ones who think so. Back in the state capital, Sangita visited the Uttar Pradesh Pollution Control Board. She met the regional officer in charge of Lucknow district. Why, she asked, are there no air pollution monitors in Sitapur district? After all, 4.5 million people live there, to say nothing of the dozens of other rural districts. Why does nobody track the rural air? 'There aren't any stations in rural India because there aren't any polluting activities there,' the officer told her. He was unmoved when Sangita presented her measurements. Rural spikes in air pollution 'only happen for a short period of time', he explained. 'Cities have pollution 365 days a year.'

Newspapers see it this way too. One series of articles is titled 'Delhi choking', a phrase with 6,780 hits in a Google search. An op-ed published in 2018 calls for policies to 'stop industries from choking… cities.' Picture air pollution in your mind. In your imagination, does it come from a factory smokestack, over a grey urban scene? The Unicode description of the factory emoji agrees: 'An industrial factory, with flue-gas stacks releasing exhaust into the air.'

Maybe everybody is right. Maybe air pollution is limited to India's cities. If rural Indians escape the pollution, all 850 million of them would have something to celebrate. And so would the rest of us: because two-thirds of Indians live outside of cities, what happens in villages is important for national statistics and for many lives.

The United Nations Population Division projects that 35 per cent of Indians will live in cities in 2020. India will be less urbanized than Bangladesh, than sub-Saharan Africa, than Asia overall, and much less than the worldwide fraction (56 per cent). Newspaper headlines proclaim 'urbanisation on the rise in India'. But the transition of India's population from rural to urban is actually happening slower than in other developing countries too. From 2015 to 2020, India will become more urban by only 2.1 percentage points. That *pace* is slower than the pace of change in Bangladesh (which is urbanising almost twice as quickly), Africa, Asia, and the world.

So, India is not only more rural than the rest of the world, it is also becoming urban more gradually. Economists Kaivan Munshi and Mark Rosenzweig have argued that India's comparatively slow urbanisation is rooted in its social inequality. Their theory is that migrants to cities sacrifice their caste-based rural social safety net. Whatever the explanation, these facts imply that rural air pollution will matter for years to come. The

UN projects that half of India's population will not live in cities until between 2045 and 2050.

Unfortunately, rural air pollution is also a fact. Nobody who has seen the picture taken from outer space of the grey clouds of smoke, reaching towards Bangladesh across the northern plains, can escape worry that hundreds of millions of rural and urban people suffer. Dr Sagnik Dey's remote sensing data confirms these fears.

The data we used for our study of child height is representative of all children born throughout India. The average rural child was born in a month with a $PM_{2.5}$ of 56. Not only is this average more than five times the WHO upper limit, it exceeds the average for urban children: 51. The average rural child inhales more pollution because the northern plains states are mostly rural, and also have worse air quality than India as a whole. The extremes are worse for rural children too: 10 per cent are born into months where the average $PM_{2.5}$ is above 115.

In Chapter 1, we saw that exposure to air pollution reduces the height of the average Indian child. With the same data, we can test whether the effects on rural and urban children differ. The focus on urban India's air pollution might be justified if a dose of airborne particles caused more harm in a city. There is no reason to suspect that this would be true. If anything, rural homes may be less likely to separate inside air from outside air. But the data let us investigate this possibility. Unsurprisingly, there is no evidence for it. The data shows that the harmful consequences of exposure to airborne particles are no different for rural and urban children.

A recent scientific paper by Alexandra Karambelas and co-authors draws the same conclusion. Karambelas' team uses a different type of data. They face the same challenge that Sangita did: 'Traditionally, surface measurements [of air pollution] reflect the best recording of ambient concentrations to determine exposure-response relationships. Yet, in India, surface monitoring is largely limited to urban regions as opposed to rural villages.' They make progress anyway by applying numerical computer models to a type of data called 'emissions inventories'. That approach combines the data they can find about the *source* activities that cause emissions. It is an alternative statistical approach that complements Sagnik's remote sensing.

Karambelas' team estimates that 3,52,400 premature adult deaths happen annually in rural India because of particulate air pollution. To compare, 1,10,800 adults prematurely die in India's cities. These mortality computations are projections, meaning that they reflect computer-simulated consequences of emissions. Observed counts of actual deaths would be even better evidence. But most deaths in India are not counted, rural deaths especially.

Getting to the source

Kanpur city is separated from rural fields only by the Ganga. Cars can cross along the top of the Ganga Barrage, a dam and tourist attraction with ice cream vendors. Air can cross anywhere. There is no kilometres-high boundary wall to divide the atmosphere at city borders. 'Air flows like a fluid', as the slogan reminds engineering students. But all that flow has to come from somewhere. I asked the engineering students' teacher where.

In the Cafe Coffee Day at the centre of the IIT-Kanpur campus, the air conditioning made such a contrast to the warm, humid outside air that condensed water ran down the windows. The staff finally solved the problem by opening wide the two glass front doors, in a seeming attempt to air condition Kanpur itself. It was summer break. Around ten or fifteen students were working silently on their laptops across the large rooms of the coffee shop. Only in the section labelled 'Silent Zone' were any of the students talking with one another.

I was there to talk with Professor Sachchida Nand Tripathi, or Sachi as he cheerfully introduced himself. We met in his office on a weekend: it seemed obvious to him that Saturday would be a work day. Perhaps he suggested the coffee shop to get away from the ringing of his office phone with requests for presentations. Sachi was once the PhD teacher of Sagnik – my collaborator who worked with Josh, Sangita, and me in Chapter 1 to learn the effect of air pollution on child height. When I visited, Sachi was part of a team that was in the final process of submitting a new research paper to a journal. His paper is one of several studies seeking to sort out where north India's air pollution comes from, based on what chemicals and particles it contains.

Many questions remain unanswered about the details of the source of north India's air pollution, even to the experts. In this, 'source apportionment' (as the experts call it) is just like every other aspect of the air pollution problem: successive central and state governments have not collected enough data or tracked the challenge. A few months before we talked, Sachi had told a reporter from Reuters, 'The state government does not have the mechanism to understand the sources of air pollution, how will they tackle it?' As Sachi explained to the reporter, the decision not to adequately investigate particulate matter cannot be excused by claiming that pollution is a surprise: 'The state needs to act. This was very much coming.'

Because high quality data is so scarce, the science is at a stage where some differences among different studies' conclusions have not been resolved. Sachi is part of one team working with the central government's pollution control board. Others use different strategies and find conclusions that are a little different.

Each strategy for source apportionment is an approach to combining incomplete data with theory and models to fill in the gaps. Some studies are bottom-up: they start with estimates of emissions, and then use a computer model to fill in how different sources of pollution would contribute to the total concentration of particles. Other studies are top-down. They look for specific chemical compounds in the final mix of particles that waft in the air. Top-down studies solve what amounts to a complex algebra problem to make the possible sources add up to the counts of fingerprint chemicals that are found in the mix. The results do not perfectly agree on the details, but both types of study find that north India's pollution comes from many sources.

What is a concerned citizen to think about all this? What does it mean when different studies give different answers about the sources of pollution? Despite the confusion, three conclusions are clear. One is that much better monitoring is necessary. Pollution levels vary radically across places and times of the year, so it would be no surprise if pollution's sources did too. It is not enough merely to track the fluctuations in the numerical levels of pollution. We also need details of the chemical make-up of the pollution that would let researchers learn more about its origins.

Sachi gave me an example: some properties of a bit of air pollution precisely reveal the process that released it. Josh Apte demonstrated a machine like this in his backyard garage. It sorts particles by giving a different electrical charge to particles depending on their mass. Grinning, Josh handed me his baby, walked around the corner, and lit a piece of paper on fire, so I could see his new apparatus blink with excitement as it cycled through its scan of particles.

Building such a system in India will require a major, sustained effort, but not an unprecedented one: other countries do it routinely. As Sachi lamented, the government bureaucrats appear to believe that they can commission a single study of source apportionment and resolve the matter, once and for all. 'There was one apportionment study done in 2014–15, and that's enough', officials seem to think. Sachi compared India with Paris and other foreign cities, where apportionment studies are continuous – 'round the clock!' – and monitoring is constant, even though air pollution levels are much lower. 'That is what they did in China', where air pollution levels used to be almost as high as India's, but have been recently brought under control.

Researchers understand this need. Almost everyone I talked with while writing this book told me about some new study to figure out the sources of Delhi's pollution. The stories often turned out to be about different members of the same few research teams. The University of Birmingham recently paid to have an article in the *Chronicle of Higher Education* advertising that their top scientists are studying Indian source apportionment: 'the university is working with partners to identify the different causes and effects of air pollution in China and India, which together account for half of all deaths linked to air pollution.'

'Great!' I thought. 'And how timely that I am writing Chapter 2.' The word 'India' is a link in that article. When I click it, the University of Birmingham website tells me that they are collaborating with engineers at IIT-Delhi, and partnering with my friend at the University of Texas. Of course, these are major research projects that need large teams. It is only good that big open questions are being tackled by international collaborations. My point is that we need many more of them, so I had hoped I would learn of something *new*. This was Sachi's point too. If in Paris – where $PM_{2.5}$ is reported to be 'good' as I type – the government monitors pollution sources round-the-clock at several sites, then India has a long way to go to build an adequate data collection network.

The second clear implication from the apportionment studies is that the air pollution comes from many sources. That means that no one quick fix will solve it all. Cars, trucks, industry, coal plants, trash burning, crop residue burning, construction, even traditional stoves and household fires to keep warm: air pollution is caused by a complex list of sources. This complexity makes it easy to appear to be taking aggressive action, without actually solving the problem. A government can highlight one small part of the problem while ignoring the rest. Even a government that wants to would be challenged to track down and plug each source of emissions in the real world where bureaucratic resources and capacity are limited.

The third upshot of the source studies is that 'Delhi's' air pollution is not only Delhi's. So, policy cannot succeed if it only focuses there. Coal burnt in Kanpur, crops burnt in Haryana, cars idling on the Gurgaon highway – each of these contributes to the pollution. Sachi implicated 'all the northern Ganga belt' as a culprit: he listed Haryana, Punjab, Delhi, UP. Getting to each source of the air pollution requires leaving Delhi. Later in the book, we will see the role of burning coal to generate electricity; for now, we will visit rural fields.

The annual apocalypse

'It looks like an apocalyptic scene. A post-war scenario. You see huge plumes of black smoke coming out. I don't know how to describe it.' My friend Avinash was telling me about seeing fields of crop residue burn in Haryana and Punjab.

Of all my friends who realized before I did that development economics is environmental economics, Avinash Kishore has been teaching me the longest. Almost fifteen years ago, we met one another first upon arriving at graduate school. We both stood flummoxed by the oversized wooden doors at the entrance to the castle where Princeton houses graduate students. We said hello.

I doubt Avinash started telling me about the importance of electricity metering for groundwater conservation that very day. But it would have started soon. A few years later, Diane and I rode with him and his parents – a party of six with the driver of the classic white Ambassador – to his family's farm land, outside of where they live in Muzaffarpur, Bihar. A coal plant is ten kilometres away. The sharecropping farmer complains to Avinash's family that he thinks the ash hurts the fields. Avinash himself grew up in a house right across a pond from the rail station, but it never occurred to him as a child to worry that it was bad for his health. 'We were just worried about it as a nuisance: the coal dust would cover our beds.'

So, Avinash has been thinking about air pollution for a while. A few years before we visited his farm, Avinash worked with us to get r.i.c.e. started as an organization. If there are any principles behind r.i.c.e.'s work, they include the importance of seeing what you are talking about in villages, and of making an opportunity to learn about something else while you are there. In the summer of 2017, Avinash was doing a survey in Punjab and Haryana about varieties of wheat and rice. He tacked on a last page of questions about crop burning.

By asking his questions in the summer, Avinash was not there for that year's season of crop burning: 'My lungs are dear to me!' But he did have going for him that farmers did not think that he was there to learn about why they burn their crops – because he was not. 'The first 45 minutes were about what wheat did you grow, why did you not change, why did you not get more yield, and then suddenly a page of questions about this.' Avinash's strategy matters because, technically, crop burning is illegal. Bans on crop burning from central and state courts have had little effect but the bans might influence how much farmers were willing to tell a surveyor. Luckily, Avinash's pages of inane seed details had established his team as harmless. Most farmers admitted to burning their crop residue even though it is illegal – a good sign that they were willing to tell him the truth.

So why do the farmers burn their crop residue, blazing their fields into an apocalyptic scene? Avinash analysed farmers' answers to the crop burning questions with Tajuddin Khan, a co-author who studies food policy. The farmers in Haryana and Punjab did not think that burning residue was a health risk, even to their own family. Avinash asked the farmers what mattered to their decision to burn their crops. Health did not register: 'When it came to air pollution, most people had rated it as low, and I think it would have been even lower' if farmers were not trying to give a polite answer.

What mattered was the simple economics. Crop residue is almost useless. 'Are you kidding me?' Avinash explained. 'A stalk is what? It's purely carbon. Carbon and a lot of moisture, and a little silica.' All that carbon, moisture and silica is just in the way of getting the next crop planted. That is expensive. 'Taking it out and dumping it has labour costs.'

But while the crop-burning apocalypse is new, the uselessness of the residue has been true for a long time. Many farmers in Haryana and Punjab can afford irrigation, so they want to clear the monsoon crop to squeeze in a winter crop. This, too, is nothing new, Avinash emphasized. 'The second crop has been around forever.'

What are changing fast are labour costs and capital costs: wages are going up in India, but machines are cheaper than ever before. Hiring workers to clear the fields is expensive. More and more farmers in Punjab and Haryana can afford combine harvesters. Unlike harvesting by hand, a combine harvester leaves stalks in the field (unless it has an attachment in the back to flatten the stalks, which combine harvesters in India typically lack). 'With manual labour, the harvesting happens closer to the root. If you go to a field that has been harvested with a combine harvester, the remaining stalk is closer to your knees.' Basmati rice, Avinash points out, is a special case, because it must be harvested by hand to remain unbroken (and saleable at high prices). Consistent with his theory, basmati fields are not usually burned.

Why would a farm owner not simply offer lower wages, offering to pay farm workers only as much as they can afford? One possibility, according to Avinash, is that workers may not take the job. Labour markets are a special type of market where the laws of supply and demand do not always apply in the ordinary way. In part, this is because the sort of job you have is a signal about what type of people you and your family are. For example, the caste-related complication of the labour market for latrine pit emptying is one reason why there is so much open defecation in rural India. Few people are willing to be hired to empty a latrine pit, a job that is unfortunately seen as ritually polluting, and is associated with the lowest social ranks. Avinash wonders if agricultural labour is coming to also be seen with stigma, as India's economy grows: 'If you stay as a farm labourer, there is no upward mobility,' a worker might reason; 'your son will not be able to become a government peon.'

But even if agricultural labour were not stigmatized, rising productivity and improving education are increasing wages. Meanwhile, more farmers can afford equipment like combine harvesters than ever before. Lighting stubble on fire remains free of (monetary) charge.

Reinvent the harvest?

The problem is economic, then. The solution, in an economics classroom, is obvious. Regulate it, tax it, do not let farmers impose this cost on everybody else. Presumably, the courts had this sort of reasoning in mind when they banned crop burning. But whether their farms were tiny, modest or large, many paddy farmers in Avinash's survey admitted to burning their crop residue anyway. When you burn your crop residue, it is obvious to everyone and sometimes visible from space. Despite crop residue burning being both illegal and obvious, there is no penalty.

It would be possible to have an effective penalty, at least in principle. Avinash gave me an example: it is illegal to transplant paddy too early in the year, because then it needs more irrigation and consumes more of the water that everybody has to share. A government order in Punjab and Haryana requires paddy farmers to wait for transplantation until closer to the monsoon, rather than the peak of summer. If you violate the order, the penalty is severe: 'They come with a tractor and plough your field back.'

It is understandable why farmers – some of whom are quite wealthy, but many of whom manage with small patches of land – would take the opportunities they have to make the money they can, without paying costs that they can avoid. Few of us go out of our way to pay costs that we do not have to. This is a classic market failure, familiar to any economics student. But when the government does not address it, it becomes a government failure too. Unfortunately, the explanation for this enduring government failure is no social scientific puzzle: farmers are politically powerful.

The only solution is to meaningfully change farmers' incentives: either by seriously penalising crop residue burning (which farmers will not like) or by implementing a subsidy or financial incentive that is only paid to growers who do not pollute the air. But such a subsidy would spend down the public purse, and will appear to some voters to reward bad behaviour. Faced with this dilemma, we might have hope for a technological escape, such as in the mechanical form of a Happy Seeder, a device that mulches the straw residue from growing rice while planting new wheat seeds at the same time.

Tajuddin and Avinash presented a summary of their research, which concludes with a dry bullet point: 'Most farmers do not know much about Happy Seeders.' They report that 'less than 10 per cent of farmers in our sample had seen a Happy Seeder or knew anyone who used one'. Among over 1,000 Punjabi farmers who they interviewed, they found about ten using a Happy Seeder.

The impulse to solve social or economic problems by inventing a new technology is a familiar one in development policy. The Bill and Melinda Gates Foundation promises to end open defecation by reinventing the toilet. For every problem, there is now a smart phone app – and a grant to fund the app's development. Technology can change people's behaviour, but only if it meaningfully changes their options. After all, farmers adopted combine harvesters because they are cheaper.

Yet, as Ridhima Gupta and E. Somanathan summarized the sobering results from a careful study of the economics of Happy Seeders: 'The gain in average profit is small and so while some farmers will see a small profit gain, others may see a small profit decline when they switch to using the new machine.' The evidence suggests that neither Happy Seeders nor any other technology will reinvent the harvest without a change in farmers' incentives.

Illness, where the wind blows it

Using fire in agriculture is nothing new. It was one of humanity's first inventions. It happens in countries all around the world. But India is not collecting the data that would allow anyone to know exactly how much harm crop burning is causing. Researchers have to fill in this blank. One strategy, which Avinash and Tajuddin tried in a further study, is to match survey data on medical treatment with estimates of crop burning from satellite measurements. They found that people are more likely to seek medical care for a respiratory infection if they live in Indian districts where crops are burned. Another strategy is to look for evidence from other countries.

That is what Marcos Rangel and Tom Vogl did. Marcos and Tom are economists who study the big picture of health and population in developing countries. Much of Tom's research asks questions about fertility: why do some mothers have more children than others? How do differences in childbearing add up to differences in education across generations? As we have seen, one of the hardest parts of studying children in developing countries is learning the basic facts. Too often, nobody ever records the data. Latin America is an exception, where recently more and more data is available than ever before. Brazil writes down the births and deaths of its children – and they suffer from agricultural fires too. So, Marcos and Tom went to the Brazilian data to sort out just how bad crop burning can be.

In the Brazilian state of São Paulo, thirteen air-monitoring stations have been collecting data for years on particulate pollution and other pollutants. São Paulo is home to 45 million people, which puts it between Odisha and Andhra Pradesh by population. The humid, monsoon, sub-tropical climate of São Paulo is classified by geographers as in the same category as Kanpur, Lucknow and Patna. Many *Paulistas* work in the urban economy of the capital city, but millions also work in sugarcane agriculture. Sugarcane growers in Brazil, like Avinash's survey respondents in Punjab, clear their fields with fire.

Marcos and Tom had data. But they still faced the fundamental statistical challenge of learning about the effects of pollution. Air pollution is not a randomized experiment, so what looks like an effect of pollution could actually be a consequence of something else. In Chapter 1, we saw that the introduction of E-ZPass to the New Jersey Turnpike was a solution to the problem that poorer (and therefore, sicker) children are likely to live in more polluted places. Marcos and Tom had an opposite problem: agricultural fires happen when and where sugarcane is being harvested. Harvest time is when farmers are paid for their crops. All that harvest money in the rural economy can be used to buy food and other things that make children better-off. So, if you are in the lucky position to be expanding the area of land that you can cultivate – or if it is the right time of the year to cash in on your crops – then two things are going on at the same time: you are going to be breathing in more smoke, while you are bringing in more cash.

How could Marcos and Tom separate the effect of the smoke from the effect of the harvest (that caused the smoke)? 'Whichever way the wind blows' is an expression for a situation that is unpredictable, maybe even random. That is exactly what they needed: an unpredictable factor that exposes some children to more air pollution than others. Luckily for Marcos and Tom, the Brazilian air monitors even recorded the direction of the wind.

So, the wind was the key to their statistical plan. At different times of year, the cycle of harvests causes fires to be more or less common in different parts of São Paulo. That is a start on a strategy, because the same families will have different children born at different times of year. Better still is that the smoke does not spread over the state. Instead, it depends on how the wind happens to blow. Two different children living in two different communities could be just as close to a fire – and just as likely to benefit from the economic effects of the harvest. But one of them is downwind from the fire and has to breathe the smoke, while the other is upwind from the fire and is spared. Because the wind can change frequently and unpredictably, otherwise comparable children could be exposed to very different levels of pollution. This is the exact situation that a population health researcher is hunting for, in a place where the data on health, pollution, and the weather are all complete enough – and in Brazil, they are.

Marcos and Tom put their plan to the test. Does the wind have such a big effect on pollution that it could make a big difference in pregnant women's exposure to smoke? It does: families who are downwind of the fires are exposed to more particles in the air. These particles then have an effect on pregnant women and on the growing foetuses they nurture. Babies in utero who had more agricultural smoke blown their mothers' way did not have as healthy of a start to life. They were born smaller and earlier, and were more likely to die, rather than be born alive.

Exposure to air pollution during pregnancy made it more likely for babies in Brazil to be born dangerously small. This makes sense biologically because air pollution makes their mothers less healthy. Then, mothers pass the deprivation on to the growing baby: mothers suffering from infections have less energy available for the baby's growth. Some scientists worry that inflammation in the lungs (as a result of air pollution) could change the cells and make-up of the blood in ways that make life riskier for the mother and the baby. Many studies, including those on the well-documented health effects of smoking cigarettes during pregnancy, show that exposure to particles in the air could make it more difficult for the mother's placenta to deliver oxygen and nutrients to the baby.

Surviving and thriving

Completing the first month of life is a statistical milestone. It means that a baby has survived the perils of neonatal mortality:

the initial month when most early-life deaths occur. The post-neonatal threats then stretch ahead for the next eleven months. Demographers distinguish deaths in these two phases of a first year because they divide cases of infant mortality roughly in half. Neonatal deaths are more likely to reflect that a baby is born too small, that its mother was undernourished, or that it did not receive the care it needed at birth. Infectious disease is implicated in many post-neonatal deaths, as slightly older babies are exposed to more of the germs in their environment. All of these challenges loom in Uttar Pradesh, where sorting out a single cause can be difficult.

In Sitapur, smoke fills a neonate's lungs from almost the beginning. If a baby is born at home, in a dark interior room, a fire is probably burning. If a baby is born anywhere during the harvest or the winter, no nearby fire is necessary to fill the air with particles.

One of Manju's triplets died a neonatal death. One morning he died, with only a few days left in his first month. Nikhil recalls Manju's early morning mobile call: he had been the biggest of the three, but he died just like that.

This book is not about his death, nor about his mother's and father's gritty struggle to keep him and his brothers safe. This book is about one of the many threats that his brothers, the ones still alive, endured despite their family's best efforts.

From 2014 to 2016, everyone at r.i.c.e. became an air pollution alarmist, each for our own reasons. Nikhil's conversion was when he understood one of Manju's dilemmas. One of the most important elements of keeping an underweight baby alive is keeping it warm. Breastfeeding is a good strategy because it shares the mother's warmth with the baby, but it does not work for three of them.

Nikhil saw that Manju had two bad options. The ordinary way for her family to keep warm was by building a fire of wood or dung, but he knew that the smoke would most likely make the babies ill. Recall the concentration-response curves from Chapter 1. In the curved supralinear case, the extra smoke from a fire might not cause so much further harm. In the dust of Sitapur, that branch of the scientific literature did not feel like anything to bet a life on.

One triplet died. Two of his brothers have survived, so far. All three suffered lasting consequences of their unhealthy start in life. The brother who died had the worst outcome. But none of them escaped, because the challenges of early childhood impact a child's body for his or her entire life.

This is the lesson of the new economics of human capital. Data is now available that links information on an adult's health or economic well-being with facts about their childhood, and even their environment before birth. Janet Currie is one of the economists who studied E-ZPass. She later worked with three other researchers to pool the evidence from more than forty studies. Each article found some way of learning about the life-long effects of pollution. For example, a paper from Israel found that students exposed to more air pollution earned lower scores on tests in schools. Another from the US found that children who were born into states and times that permitted leaded gasoline went on to have more behavioural problems, years later.

How much a child weighs at birth is particularly important in predicting its future. In Brazil, the data showed that exposure to agricultural smoke caused babies to be born smaller. Smaller babies are more likely to die. Babies who weigh more at birth are not only more likely to live: on average, they go on to receive more education and earn more money. The effects on any one child are small, but they matter in the whole population.

The consequences of early-life persist because our bodies persist. Children's bodies grow and develop differently if they are exposed to more pollution. The effects can endure into old age. They begin as early as in the womb. So, people with an unhealthy early start in life earn less money and die earlier, on average. In fact, the effect does not even stop within a lifetime. Mothers who grew up in more polluted environments are themselves more likely to give birth to low birth-weight children, passing the burden on to the next generation.

Dora Costa, an economic demographer, argues that such patterns were an important part of the development and history of inequality in the United States. She is interested in the time when the US faced many of the challenges that developing countries face today, including births at home. Like in poor populations now, most births and deaths were not tabulated by any statistical agency. Costa found records from the New York Lying-In hospital, a place built in 1902 where women could give birth other than at home. New York Lying-In wrote down birth weights.

At least in this data, birth weights were much more dispersed by income levels than they are today. In Lying-In, a baby at the 90th percentile weighed 118 grams at birth more than a baby at the 10th percentile. Nation-wide, the gap would have been even larger than it was within this one New York hospital. But by 1988, this difference was only 52 grams, in a sample representative of the US. As Costa reminds us, 'Advances in obstetrical, medical, and nutritional knowledge have come slowly and progress has not always been linear.' Progress can reverse – for example, if India reduces exposure to open defecation while also permitting air pollution to increase. The point is that increasing equality by improving health at birth can be *cumulative*. The gap between the worst-off and the best-off can narrow over time as healthier babies grow up to be healthier parents.

Babies' lesson for economists

Because of the economics of human capital, India's babies have a new perspective to bring to the old debate between development and the environment. Recall the paradox from Chapter 1. There is no ambiguity in the economics profession's understanding that air pollution is a classic market failure. Still, it sounds wise and statesmanlike to gravely regret that economics is the enemy of the environment. According to this view, preventing unhealthy air pollution would be nice to have, but a poor developing country cannot afford it.

What explains this conflict between clear economics and confused policy? One possibility is that wealthy interests are able to pay some economists to muddle the debate – to argue in a way that confuses the goals of particular corporations for the benefits that the market can bring everybody. This surely happens: public debates include voices that are not speaking for the public interest.

It also happens that some voices are excluded from public debates. These arguments – market efficiency versus market failure, free enterprise versus government regulation – have been at the heart of debates in philosophy, politics, and economics for centuries. Economists and ethicists imagine a society of individuals with different resources and talents. Who should get what, we wonder? How should society decide? Should we trade, vote, regulate, or fight it out?

What we now know is that this standard fable leaves somebody out of the grand council: babies. (In fact, it has historically left a lot of people out, although the circle is slowly expanding.) In this classic thought experiment, we imagine that the rules for an economy are being designed by a group of unequal earners. The important question is to decide how much taxes should be, how generous public benefits should be. Somehow, everyone in this imaginary economic state of nature is one of the adults alive today. The social contract has no signatories from the next generation. Children do not get to vote. A foetus in utero does not have purchasing power.

It is time for effects on children and infants to be added to economists' standard list of market failures. The textbooks can call it 'intergenerational externalities'. An externality is a case where a decision has effects on other people that are not taken into account by the decision-maker. Intergenerational externalities are one of those cases. Economists shrug this possibility off: parents care about their children, so standard practice in economic theory is to model households as infinitely-lived dynasties. In these models, economic decision-makers may be impatient, but because they live forever (by assumption!) they perfectly integrate the hopes and fears of every generation. But nobody really knows or thinks about their descendants that far in the future – and too few people care.

It is time for these assumptions to change. Behavioural experiments have forced economists to accept that we humans do not take decisions according to the rational rules of probability – as standard mathematical models assume. We are also not infinitely-lived dynasties. Sometimes, it may be good enough to write an economic theory under the convenient fiction that the interests of adults are identical to the interests of children, babies, and foetuses. The lesson that babies have for economists, however, is that often such a theory will not be good enough, because health in early life turns out to be very important.

Scientists now understand that what happens at the beginning of life stays with us until the end. So, the lessons of early-life human capital tell us to set aside the old debate on economic development versus the environment. Economists now know that economic development is, at its heart, an *intergenerational* process. Today's workers invest in their children's nutrition and health. Today's taxes pay for public health initiatives, sanitation, and infrastructure that bring children into a healthier environment.

Then, those children grow up to be the next generation: on average a little bit healthier, a little bit smarter, and a little bit more productive. In the introduction, I said that particle pollution was a short-term problem, compared to the long-term horizon of climate change. But in that, I was incomplete. The intergenerational replacement of human bodies with ever-slightly-better early-life conditions is an upwards cycle of prosperity – unless impediments such as polluting environments, unsanitary disease, or undernourished mothers get in the way. Human development is a mechanism of economic development, so children are one of a country's most important capital stocks.

3

Homes and Kitchens

'Imagine two villages. In one of them, everybody defecates in the open. In the other one, everybody uses a latrine. In which village do you think children would be healthier, or would they be the same?'

The r.i.c.e. team asked this question to over 3,000 people in 2013 and 2014, trying to understand why open defecation in rural India is declining so slowly. To many villagers the answer was obvious: open defecation is the wholesome choice, out in the village air! Others thought it did not make a big difference. Forty-three per cent of respondents said that open defecation is at least as healthy as latrine use. Only 57 per cent thought that latrine use would be better for children's health.

In September of 2013, I sat next to Kailash under a thatched awning in Sitapur, listening as he led a respondent through the questions. I was sitting on a grain sack that I had brought, to help the respondent feel comfortable about me being with him on the ground. My attention was focused on trying not to seem too interested in this particular survey question. We were testing our survey script and training our surveyors. I knew that we were making progress when I heard villagers telling us that open defecation was the healthier choice.

The challenge is that the people we met in villages – the ones who we annoyed with our long list of questions – were trying to be nice to us and to our surveyors. We were all educated visitors from a city, writing on clipboards. To be part of our interviewer team, you have to be willing to sit on the ground with respondents, to speak gently, and to listen earnestly. But even the best surveyors cannot fully overcome the fact that a polite respondent will tell the surveyor what he or she imagines (rightly or wrongly) that the surveyor wants to hear.

The only solution is to confuse the matter and obscure what we want to hear. In the sanitation survey – the one that we did because we were interested in open defecation – we told villagers that we wanted to learn all about village life. And we asked all about village life! Like in Avinash's study of crop varieties, the surveyors did not start out by asking whether open defecation or latrine use was healthier. They began by asking respondents to imagine two villages, one where everyone eats rice and one where everyone eats wheat. Which one would be healthier? We were doing our survey in north India, so the village that ate rotis was the clear winner.

Then they asked about two imaginary villages, one in which everybody cooks with kerosene and one in which everybody cooks on a traditional stove. In which village would children be healthier? A stupefying 88 per cent of villagers chose traditional stoves: hearty, wholesome village food, cooked right on an open fire is what growing children need, they said.

Smelling the neighbours' cooking

Unfortunately, the people who told our surveyors this were wrong. If everyone in a village burns wood and dung to cook, instead of using LPG, the smoke will pollute the air that children breathe. Sagnik's data from space told us that rural people – and not only urban people – live with air pollution. Burning dung and wood to cook happens in rural and urban homes. Especially for rural children, cooking is a source of air pollution that happens right at home. Three-fourths of rural Indian households cook by burning traditional fuel, demographic data from 2015 and 2016 finds. This produces what scientists call 'household' air pollution, as distinct from 'ambient' air pollution – the background particles that float in the air for everybody.

Aashish Gupta and I were on the same field team during the sanitation survey. Our days started in neighbouring sleeping bags. We rode jeeps out together to ask all these questions about village life. When we finished the survey, Aashish started a PhD in demography at Penn. For his dissertation, he decided to find out whether the villagers were right. What actually are the consequences on the health of a village where everybody cooks on a traditional stove?

Other researchers had already compared children living in households with and without clean cooking fuel. The stove makes a big difference. A study in Guatemala, for example, compared babies born to mothers who cooked by burning traditional fuel with babies born to mothers who had been randomly selected to receive a chimney stove. The chimney redirected the smoke away from the pregnant mother. The babies born to the mother with the reduced-smoke stove weighed more when they were born, on average, although the effects were clearest for infants born in the cold season. The senior author on this study was Kirk Smith, a scientist who has studied air pollution in populations around the world. In Zimbabwe, another team that Smith worked with found that babies born to mothers who burned solid fuel like wood or dung were born smaller than babies born to mothers using LPG or other clean fuels. Likewise, in Nepal: women exposed to air pollution from burning traditional fuel were more likely to get tuberculosis.

Study after study finds that some of the most polluted air anywhere is what rural women breathe while cooking inside their own homes. An even more detailed experimental study is currently underway in four developing countries. Its goal is to learn the effect on children of providing stoves to pregnant women. This experiment, led by Tom Clasen, is randomized. So, its conclusions will not be threatened by any possibility that women with clean cooking fuel are richer or otherwise healthier.

Aashish, however, was interested in a different question: what about the neighbours? Existing research had compared the health of women and families with clean fuel to the health of women and families with traditional fuel. But Aashish had seen the *village-wide* effects of open defecation, from his work on sanitation: when germs spread throughout the village, they make everyone sick. Could air pollution work the same way? Smoke spreads throughout a village, even if it is most concentrated in the kitchen that generates it. So, village-wide consequences of burning dung and wood seemed possible too.

To investigate this question, Aashish would need a big dataset. He was not merely comparing one *family* to another. He was comparing one *village* to another, so an entire village would only count as one small point in his statistics. Moreover, he needed all types of villages: villages where most people burned dung and wood, villages where most people burn LPG and clean fuels, and villages at all the steps along the way in between.

Fortunately, Aashish was being trained as a demographer. Demographers study large datasets that reveal patterns about an entire population. So, Aashish was able to find just the survey data he needed, with information on the health of a sample of almost ten thousand Indians. He found data that included measurements of lung function: 9,551 participants blew into a machine that measured the volume of air that their lungs could move. If air pollution mattered for respiratory health, this would be the data that could reveal the consequences.

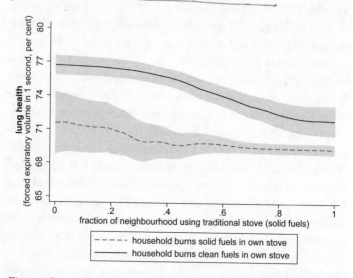

Figure 8. In a village where more families cook with traditional fuel, everyone's lungs are hurt

Figure 8 plots what Aashish discovered. Along the horizontal axis is the fraction of a village that uses LPG or other clean cooking fuels: in villages on the right, everybody cooks on LPG or something similar, while in villages on the left, everybody cooks on something smoky like dung or wood. The vertical axis is Aashish's measure of lung function: bigger numbers mean healthier lungs that can move more air. There are two lines to keep separate the families that use traditional fuel from the households that have made the switch to LPG and clean cooking fuel. We already know from the work of Kirk Smith and other researchers that a family's health tends to be worse if it uses traditional fuel. So, it is no surprise that the two lines are vertically distant from one another. Part of this vertical distance is the poor health that a family suffers when it breathes its own smoke.

But what about the smoke of others? Its effects are visible in the slant of both lines. That slant means that how your neighbours cook matters. Whether a family uses LPG or traditional fuels, there will be healthier outcomes, on average, if it lives in a village where fewer households' cooking pollutes the air with smoke. This was the core discovery of Aashish's research. It remained after his statistical verifications that his analysis of different villages credibly compared apples to apples. Air pollution is a problem for everyone.

If traditional cooking fuel does so much harm, it is important to know why families choose it. An obvious explanation would appear to be poverty. Yet, rural India's transition to clean cooking fuel has been slow, even despite economic growth. In India's 2015–16 Demographic and Health Survey, 75 per cent of households burned solid fuel for cooking. This figure has been improving, but the decline is slow. Traditional fuel use is down only 15 percentage points from a decade before, when the figure exceeded 90 per cent. Moreover, much solid fuel use remains.

Economists Rema Hanna and Paulina Oliva tested poverty as an explanation for traditional fuel use. They used data from an experiment in West Bengal. In the experiment, some families were made less poor: they were given money and animals, including cows and goats. Hanna and Oliva computed whether becoming less poor made families more likely to switch away from solid fuel.

They found that the *opposite* happened. 'Households did not switch to a better cooking source and, in fact, many switched to a worse, but more readily available source – the assets that are in the form of livestock produced a cheap source of dung for fuel use.' In another experiment, Hanna and her co-authors found an even more direct result: when a non-profit organization gave almost-free stoves to families in Odisha villages, the families simply did not use them. 'Households used the stoves irregularly and inappropriately, failed to maintain them, and usage declined over time,' the researchers concluded. What explains such apparent indifference to smoky air and the harm it causes?

Stoves and status

'If men did the cooking, the switch would happen overnight,' Avinash hypothesized. This conversation happened not so many years after Avinash and I first met at Princeton's forbidding castle doors. We were both still PhD students. We were thinking through what would become one of our first collaborations. Avinash's suggestion was that the problem is that women lack power and rank last within rural families. Women collect the fuel and hunch over the stove. They are the first to breathe the smoke. But whether to get an LPG connection or pay to refill a cylinder is not their decision – such an expense would be for a man to decide.

'We had only one cylinder,' Avinash recalled about his childhood mixture of fuel sources. 'Those were the days when you needed a Member of Parliament to get a second cylinder. My mom and aunt used to cook on LPG during the day and chulha at night. We also had an electric heater, a kerosene stove: fuel was a big headache.'

Aashish's research already showed that smoky stoves make a situation that economists call an externality. In an externality, the person who bears the harms is different from the person who makes the decision. Traditional stoves create an externality because one household's stove can contribute to making the rest of the village unhealthy. Avinash's hypothesis would add to the externality, because women breathe in the consequences of men's decisions. In other words, overuse of traditional cooking fuel would be a case of an economic inefficiency caused by social inequality.

Of course, women are not the only ones living in villages who breathe the smoke from traditional stoves. Everybody does, although men inhale less of it and at a greater distance. More importantly, everybody starts out a foetus, surviving and thriving only as well as their mothers' bodies allow. So, every Indian, male or female, whose mother or neighbours used a traditional stove was harmed by the fact that women often do not get to choose. Traditional stoves, then, are an intergenerational externality too.

Paradoxically, this means that discrimination does not discriminate in its effects. Everyone is harmed, because early-life development matters for everyone. Everyone has a mother. Cooking fuel is one way that inequality turns out to cause indiscriminate harm.

If Avinash's conjecture were right – if it were true that India's slow switch to clean cooking fuel is rooted in the social disadvantage of women – then we would have learned something important about why village air stays smoky, and whether it is likely to change. But we quickly accepted that his idea would be a difficult hypothesis to use statistics to test. The difficulty is that women with more decision-making power are different from women with less decision-making power in many ways, beyond merely their cooking fuel use.

Consider what such a statistical study might look like. A researcher could come up with a measure of women's empowerment. For example, a standard question included in many surveys is whether women get to decide what to cook or what to buy without asking their husband's or other family members' permission. Then, the researcher could compare whether women with more decision-making power are more likely to use LPG. Are women with less decision-making power more likely to cook on wood or dung?

Avinash and I started with that comparison. The result was what we expected. Families where the women got to make more decisions about where to go and what to do were about three times as likely to use LPG as families where the women did not get to make many decisions. But what did we learn? If more empowered women were more likely to get to use LPG, this is the sort of pattern that we would expect. Yet, the same pattern could happen for other reasons too. Maybe what really matters, for example, is education. Better-educated women are more likely to understand the health hazards of burning dung; they also are more likely to assert themselves in decision-making. Or, maybe it is just about poverty. LPG costs money, and the sort of places in India where women are the least empowered tend to also be, on average, the places where people are poorest.

We had a puzzle. Too often, women are not the ones who make purchasing decisions. But how could we test whether slow adoption of clean cooking fuel is caused, in part, by women's low social status – without being misled by the fact that socially disadvantaged women also tend to be poorer, less well educated, and in less urbanized places? We were back to the basic dilemma of econometrics: we want to know the effect of women's empowerment, but we cannot run an experiment to disempower women. We needed to find a reason that women's status varies across families that we could learn from. We needed a proxy for power that would not merely replicate the distinctions of wealth or education.

Female disadvantage, unfortunately, extends across generations. Women are discriminated against; their daughters are discriminated against; and mothers' treatment, in turn, depends on whether they are lucky enough to give birth to a boy, instead of a girl. Patricia Jeffery and co-authors recount a birth in rural Uttar Pradesh. Patricia, the mother-in-law, and the midwife wait through the night in the smoky, muddy back room. The baby turns out to be a girl: 'after a boy's birth, there would have been celebrations, presents, and jollity, so this birth is a disappointment.' The new mother is 'plaintive'; the midwife blames God. Afterward, the mother-in-law of the woman who gave birth offers a smaller-than-usual payment to the midwife, explaining 'it would be different for a boy'.

It would have been different for the mother, too. We found that women whose first-born child was a boy go on to have an improvement in their social status, relative to women whose first-born child is a girl. Avinash's family is what made him imagine that women's status might be part of the explanation for the endurance of traditional fuels. It also gave him an idea for how to study women's status: compare mothers who first had boys with mothers who first had girls. 'My paternal grandmother loved my dad,' Avinash remembered. 'She was upfront about it. She would not hide it. She told us that only when he was born did she get a backbone. Having a son gave me *bal*' – Avinash paused to translate the word for me – 'strength'.

Like for Avinash's father's mother, having a boy strengthens women's backbones. For example, data shows that women who have a boy first go on to have more body mass, relative to their height. More body mass is a good sign of improved conditions for the average mother in India, because so many are dangerously underweight.

Avinash and I only looked at the consequences of the sex of first-born children, not every child. This is because we wanted a clean experiment to test our hypothesis. Some parents in India have sex-selective abortions, meaning that they abort girl foetuses because they are girls. But sex-selective abortion is much less likely for a first birth. So, we had something close to a randomized experiment. We also looked only at urban families. In our data from the 1990s and 2000s, about half of urban households used clean cooking fuel, but only a very few rural households did. For rural households, in those days, clean cooking fuel was so uncommon that women's status was not the most important issue.

What patterns in the data would have been evidence for our views? What if Avinash's hypothesis about women's decision-making power was right? Then, because a woman's social status is improved if her first child is a boy, we would expect to find that women whose first child was a boy are more likely to use clean cooking fuel than women whose first child was a girl. That is exactly what the data showed. Richer mothers were more likely to enjoy clean cooking fuel than poorer mothers. But across the economic spectrum, there is about a three-percentage point difference, based on the sex of the first-born child. Mothers with a first boy are more likely to subsequently switch away from traditional fuel.

Among the factors that matter for fuel choice, the sex of first-born children is not the most important. Three percentage points is not a large effect. But the point is not the randomisation of boys and girls. The point is what it stands for, the processes that it reveals: social inequality and discrimination against mothers are among the factors that keep everyone in India's villages breathing in their neighbours' polluting smoke. If sex discrimination did not matter for how families make decisions, then the random sex of a baby would not predict which fuel they use to cook.

Discrimination and democracy

Discriminatory treatment of women, and especially young mothers, is improving in India. It still has a long way to go. In surveys conducted in 2016 and 2017, and representative of adults in Delhi, Mumbai, Rajasthan, and UP, about half of respondents disapproved of married women working outside the home, if their husbands can earn a good living. Most Hindu women reported practising *ghunghat*, covering their faces. Even in Delhi, three-fourths of women aged 18 to 25 do. Many women in many households across India eat their meals only after the men have. So, if women's low social position is one reason that smoke remains from burning wood and dung, the air is unlikely to fully clear for a long time.

One promising change is the Ujjwala programme: a prominent scheme of the central government, which has been distributing LPG cylinders. Manju, the mother of the triplets, was one of the many women across UP who received clean cooking fuel before the recent state elections. A classic tale about Indian elections is that politicians do nothing but give away TVs and alcohol immediately before elections. I have never personally seen one of those TVs, and I doubt politics ever hinged on TV bribes. But if it did, buying votes with LPG cylinders would be a big improvement.

In their fieldwork across UP and rural north India, my collaborators tell me that they indeed find women using their Ujjwala cylinders. Some people, though, worry about whether they will be able to refill their tanks when they run out. So, most families, even with Ujjwala cylinders, still burn some dung or wood each day. Many women who cook on a gas stove can now cook standing up, rather than squatting over a fire on the ground. Their posture embodies an improvement in their position. And, the air is healthier for everybody to breathe. If politicians are rewarded with votes for distributing something that people want, that improves social equality, and that simultaneously replaces a negative health externality with the public good of clean air, then perhaps democracy has something going for it, after all.

As I write this, the Bharatiya Janata Party (BJP) has released an election video celebrating their achievements. The video combines moving images with quantitative claims about public management and problems solved. In a charming scene, an adult son comes home from his migrant work, all smiles on the long-haul state bus ride. His heart is warmed by the benefits of his mother's Ujjwala cylinder: she has clean hands and cooks standing up. The video does not ask why the family waited for the government to give her an LPG cylinder instead of buying one.

Instead, the movie offers an accomplishment for everyone: electricity, roads, passports, forms, by the thousands, crore, or kilometre, as appropriate. The video testifies to a democratic government that is in touch with what the population wants – and is ready to deploy numbers and modern management to deliver it. This would be a serious step up from alcohol and TVs. But few voters would be very likely to change their vote because of air pollution statistics, which are not among the video's factoids.

In the last scenes, the Indian prime minister waves from the back of a car, then brings his hands together in a bow. Because this book goes to press in May 2019, I do not know if this video helped the PM win a second term in office. Nor will anybody know by the time this book is published whether Manju's Ujjwala cylinder was ever refilled – or if she was confident enough that a refill would be available to ever use all of the fuel.

More importantly, nobody knows whether elections are a system that can manage a problem like air pollution. It is hard to make a moving video about a coal plant that was not built; a field of stubble that was never burnt; a car inspection that found an emissions violation. Would such a video change any votes? Elections can be good at giving people some things they want, for some amount of time – electricity subsidies are a clear example, as we will find in the next chapter. But no prior democracy has ever been as polluted as the air is now in India's rural villages.

PART II
The Long Run

4

Electricity and Economics

'Pollution should never be the price of prosperity.' So says a sign in the waiting room of Goa's Dabolim Airport. This is easy for Goans to say: in Goa, infant mortality is low, literacy rates are high, and the sky is clear. The most polluted parts of India are the rural northern plains; these are not the prosperous states of India. Evidently, in Delhi and the northern plains, decision makers have disagreed with the airport sign's priorities.

Indira Gandhi did so most famously: 'Are not poverty and need the greatest polluters?' she asked the UN Conference on the Environment. Gandhi grew up in Allahabad, which one website claims has a $PM_{2.5}$ over 600 as I write in December 2018. Of course, it would have had cleaner air in her 1920s childhood. Even in 1972, environmental issues might have seemed like unnecessary luxuries – especially in contrast with the needs of the poor. That was the year Gandhi addressed the UN Conference in Stockholm as India's prime minister.

Gandhi's speech is remembered as an early and decisive statement of the view that poor countries should not be expected to divert resources towards environmental preservation. Norman Borlaug, who won the Nobel Peace Prize for his contributions to the Green Revolution, wrote to agree. 'I want to congratulate you for the strong position you took at Stockholm defending the rights of developing countries of the world to use science and technology to improve the standard of living of their people.'

Part I of this book focused on India's short-term challenges from particle pollution. Part II turns towards further horizons. Over the long term, one of the most important fountains of well-being is sustained economic growth. Gandhi was not alone among developing country leaders in worrying that stewarding the environment might not be worth the economic costs. So, this chapter changes focus from the costs of pollution to the costs of avoiding pollution. In the next two chapters, we assemble the models that economists have built to compare these costs and benefits.

To an economist, the cost of something is what you give up in order to get it. Much of India's air pollution is a by-product of generating electricity. If Indians had to give up the goal of electrifying the homes of the poor, then protecting India's children from polluted air would be very costly. But in fact, this is not the cost. Moreover, the way that India generates its electricity now contributes to another cost to its long-run well-being: climate change, the topics of Chapters 5 and 6. This chapter focuses on electricity and the economy: what do Indians, especially the poor, have to give up for a healthier environment?

❧

Should developing countries invest in environmental health? Must using 'science and technology' harm the environment, as Borlaug seemed to assume? Debates endured long after Gandhi's speech. The evidence from the last few chapters demonstrated the importance of intergenerational externalities. The economics of human capital agrees with the sign at the Goa airport: pollution does not promote prosperity, but instead saps children's embodied human capital.

This chapter returns to the original economic motivation for the apparent conflict. Whether Indira Gandhi was right or wrong in 1972, our job is to ask a different question: is she right today, almost fifty years later? The Government of India's Performance Dashboard (which came to me through a paid online advertisement) is a website that displays a grid of swiftly scrolling digits. Today, these include 'No. of Un-electrified Villages: 0' and 'Households Electrified under Saubhagya since Oct. 2017: 24,024,912'. Independent survey data largely agrees: by now, India is getting closer to every family receiving some electricity. So, maybe things are different than they were in the 1970s. Can some Indians now afford to care about the environment, even though many people are still poor?

What about the importance for economic development of energy? What about the fact that even families who receive some electricity do not receive enough? It would be absurd to deny that electrification improves the lives of the families who enjoy it. So, this chapter begins by taking a break from documenting the costs of air pollution to emphasize the undeniable benefits of modern energy. But what exactly do these benefits imply? Neither that poverty is always what blocks faster electrification, nor that energy scarcity is responsible for India's most important human development challenges. Economic lives are changing quickly – it is time for environmental debates to catch up with the facts.

Electrification improves lives

Richer countries consume more electricity. Comparing countries around the world, an unmistakable pattern links economic wealth and electrification. Consider two countries at different levels of economic development. The average ratio of their GDPs per capita is tightly linked to the ratio of their electricity consumption per capita. Indeed, countries appear to line up in rough formation in a data plot.

That pattern is important. It reminds us that modern economic development and electrification go hand and hand. Still, such a pattern could exist for many reasons. It could be that richer countries decided to invest their extra wealth in electrification. It could be that electrical power is a necessary ingredient in producing economic growth. Or, both of these processes could be at work at different times or in different places. We risk drawing the wrong lesson about what to do if we do not take the care to understand why this pattern emerges.

Correlations across countries are difficult to understand. Often, there are too many differences among Senegal, India, China and Belgium to be certain of any one account. So, to understand why economic development and electrification appear together, economists have turned to household-level statistics within countries. Such studies build towards a larger answer by answering smaller questions convincingly. As in population health, the trick is to find the cases that a careful study can learn from.

A year before the end of apartheid in South Africa, two-thirds of households lacked electricity. In the next seven years, fully a quarter of South African households were connected to the electrical grid. Taryn Dinkleman is an economist from South Africa. She understood that such a large, rapid change gave an opportunity to learn about the benefits of electrification for the poor.

Electrification allowed 15,000 women in rural South Africa to join the labour force and earn an income. Now that women were connected to the grid, they could cook and light their homes with electricity. They no longer had to spend time finding and burning wood. They could use that time earning money.

Dinkleman also found that women's wages went down a little, on average, when electrification came. The change in wages was not large. It does not imply that the average woman was worse off. To the contrary, it reflects the fact that more women were able to sell labour and earn income. They were freed from the drudgery of traditional fuels. The combination of outcomes – substantially more employment, slightly lower wages, much less wood burning – together tell of better lives.

In Kenya, no sudden collapse of apartheid was available to generate a surprising statistical change in electrification. Instead, electrification there has a different unexpected feature. Many families are *nearly* electrified, but not quite actually connected. They live under the grid, but their house is not attached to the wires overhead. Kenneth Lee and his economist co-authors noticed this situation. They wondered if it presented a quick-win opportunity to improve lives cheaply.

The economists organized an experiment. Different families were offered connections to the nearby electrical grid at different, randomly assigned prices. The goal was to learn how much Kenyans were willing and able to pay for electrical connections. To economists, this is a way to learn how policymakers should value and prioritize an improvement. Lee's team found that, on average, households were not ready to pay enough to cover the costs of their house being connected. If not, it is unsurprising that they remain unattached and under the grid.

It is possible that both these investigations are correct. On the one hand, electrification made households in South Africa better off in part by promoting women's opportunities to earn money. (In India, where social attitudes keep many women from working for pay, electrification probably would not have the same average effect.) But on the other hand, households in Kenya might not have the ready cash to pay for electrification's benefits. Under-grid Kenyans, moreover, may be glad that their villages are connected, even if their own house is not. They may enjoy public lights, or poles that can charge a mobile phone. By design, the Kenyan experiment did not investigate big picture changes, such as when electricity powers a new factory that creates new jobs.

Economists will debate the details. Still, nobody argues that it does not make a family better off to have a light bulb at night, a fan in the heat, or a refrigerator to store food. Moreover, none of these accounts capture the full consequences for everybody in society: it makes you better off if my child can study at night, or if electricity helps me start a business to sell a product that you want to buy.

'Electricity is life' was the simple summary offered to me by one villager living near a coal plant in UP. In some ways, he was literally correct. Exposure to extreme heat can be deadly, especially during a sudden heat wave. Statistics on mortality and extreme weather in the historical US show that the spread of air conditioning played an important role in dampening the deadly association between heat and death among the elderly. Mortality from high temperatures will become ever more important as climate change progresses. Electricity's benefits are too large and too obvious to deny.

∾

Kanpur's struggles for electrification are dramatized in the 2013 documentary film *Katiyabaaz*. 'Katiya' are illegal bits of wire that are used to steal electricity from the grid. In the Sitapur neighbourhood where Diane and I lived, children would pass the warning when the police were coming. Neighbour after neighbour would pull down their illicit katiya before they could be caught. A katiyabaaz is a specialist in the business of attaching those bits of wire. In Kanpur, he is the hero of the movie and of the neighbourhood. His fingers may be bent and burnt from close calls with the electrical current. To the tailors and businessmen who hire him, these are merely the badges of the katiyabaaz's public service.

Perhaps the most powerless person in the movie is the highest-ranking government officer: the Indian Administrative Service bureaucrat who is assigned to be managing director (MD) of the Kanpur electricity distribution company. As she explains to anybody who will listen, lost revenue from stolen electricity deprives the government of the funds needed to replace tangles of illicit wires with a legal grid. She resolves to fight back against electricity theft. But the only tool she has, sitting in her wood-panelled meeting room, is to order her middle managers to crack down. So, the teams of executives and police officers drive about, taking pictures with their phones and issuing fines. The fines are appealed and little changes.

Although the movie does not include them, one of the MD's reforms was to introduce new metering technology that is more difficult to circumvent. According to the *Hindu*, her efforts saved the distribution company money: 'the losses almost halved'. In the process, she made enemies – and not only of the katiyabaaz, who does not spare the camera his foul opinions of the company.

The climax of the movie is the 2012 Uttar Pradesh election. An up-and-coming MLA candidate from the Samajwadi Party makes a show of yelling at the administrator about electricity prices and cuts. He gets himself arrested for intimidating a public servant – and therefore gets himself on TV. He and his party eventually win the state elections, so the MD is sent to be district magistrate of Pilibhit, a district on the distant border with Nepal. The katiyabaaz continues his work.

The movie never depicts the higher power. The audience does not see the coal plants and other generators that determine how much electricity the MD receives to distribute, nor the decision makers, who decide how much generation capacity will be built. Because the katiyabaaz focused on the visible enemy – the MD and the fees she collects – he overlooked the political choices that electrify his and Kanpur's economy.

The Great Escape from 1972

The global economy has changed in the fifty-odd years since Indira Gandhi's speech. We can understand the perspective of an Indian Prime Minister during the 1972 speech, or even the 1992 Rio Earth Summit. At that time, a reasonable position to take would be that richer countries could afford to take care of the environment, but India could not. When India became as well-off as Sweden (where Gandhi spoke) or as other rich countries, then India too should invest in clearing its air.

Statistically, that day may have come. The average Indian is still poorer than the average Swede. But setting aside money, life expectancy – arguably an indicator of what matters most – has been converging around the world. Figure 9 plots this key dimension of India's human development, from the 1960s (when Gandhi was first Prime Minister) to the present. The vertical axis is life expectancy at birth, a core measure of the well-being of a population. The horizontal lines plot the levels that developed countries enjoyed when the environmental debates of the 20th century were first taking shape. (Although they too have improved since then, the global gaps have narrowed).

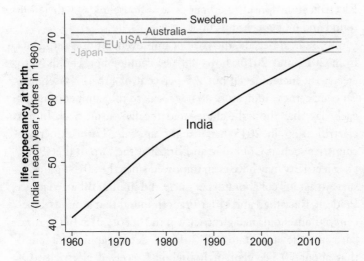

Figure 9. Life expectancy in India has caught up to where rich countries were when environmental challenges were first understood

What Figure 9 reveals is that in some important ways, India is catching up with where richer countries used to be, at key historical points in the debate between the environment and the economy. 'It will be time to sacrifice when we are as well-off as Sweden is' may have been a justified attitude in 1972. If so, it may now be time that some people in India can afford to invest in the environment.

Recall the Great Escape from the Introduction: Angus Deaton's name for the bundle of improvements that are transforming an ever-richer, healthier, safer developing world. The Great Escape includes electrification. In India's first Demographic and Health Survey in 1992, only 51 per cent of households had electricity.

Electrification spread to 60 per cent of households by the 1998 round and 68 per cent by 2005.

In the next decade, the pace of improvement doubled. Data from 2015 and 2016 shows 88 per cent of households with electricity, including all but 2.5 per cent of urban households. Of course, these indicators do not speak to the number of hours each day that the light shines and the fan turns. Still, India's electrification in 2015 had caught up with Latin American countries such as Colombia and Brazil at the turn of the 1990s.

Electricity may have even improved since the 2016 figures. A survey that my collaborators at r.i.c.e. did in rural Bihar, Madhya Pradesh, Rajasthan and Uttar Pradesh found that around 90 per cent of households had electricity in the fall of 2018. In the rural parts of these same states, the 2015–16 demographic data found that about 70 per cent of households received electricity. Of course, even if the figure is now 90 per cent or more, almost all of these families still live with power cuts. But by all accounts, access is improving fast.

These changes are visible in the night light of Kanpur. The past three decades have brought a major improvement from the situation chronicled by the 1989 Kanpur *District Gazette*. It reports, under the heading 'Street Lighting': 'The town is electrified by approximately 5000 electric posts.' The next page continues this theme: 'Special Achievements – There is hardly any town planning in the city of Kanpur.' We should not tailor today's environmental policy for the Kanpur of 1989.

Even more important than economic improvements have been the ongoing Great Escapes from early mortality and disease. The duel between economic development and environmental stewardship misleads each side into denying impressive facts: either a denial that electrification brings needed benefits, or a denial that economic transformations have already occurred. It does not serve the interests of the poor for the 2019 left to recycle images of 1970s poverty, or to ignore the forces (including market forces) that have made lives so much better. And yet, it also does not serve society's interest in economic progress and efficiency for the right to ignore market failures such as air pollution or intergenerational externalities, or to assume that economic development will fix problems that arise from externalities.

How humanity escaped the population bomb

'If I were a gambler, I would take even money that England will not exist in the year 2000.'

Paul Ehrlich would have lost that bet. Ehrlich is a biologist who has long warned about the dangers of overpopulation. In 1968, Ehrlich published *The Population Bomb*, a book that raised the alarm about the high fertility rates of the mid-20th century: 'The battle to feed all of humanity is over. In the 1970s, hundreds of millions of people will starve to death in spite of any crash programs embarked upon now. At this late date, nothing can prevent a substantial increase in the world death rate.' In case anyone finds my book alarmist, I have to mention that those were the *first words* of Ehrlich's – in the edition published four years before Indira Gandhi's Stockholm speech.

Ehrlich never actually formed a bet about the existence of England. But in 1980, Julian Simon, a business professor, found a way to take Ehrlich up on the principle of the wager. Simon contacted Ehrlich, offering 'to stake US$10,000... on my belief that the cost of non-government-controlled raw materials (including grain and oil) will not rise in the long run'. Under the terms of the deal, Ehrlich would be allowed to choose any raw materials he wanted and any date more than a year away. Ehrlich selected copper, chromium, nickel, tin, and tungsten. Simon would win if, on 29 September 1990, the inflation-adjusted price of these five commodities was lower than it was in 1980. Ehrlich would win if the inflation-adjusted prices went up.

The price of tungsten was not really what the bet was about. The bet was about whether humanity was running out of what it needed. Ehrlich worried that there were too many of us, that people were consuming more and more, and that there was only so much tungsten in the ground to be mined. In economists' language, population growth and overconsumption were shifting out the demand curve. With increasing demand and a fixed global supply of resources, the price would have to go up.

Simon believed that Ehrlich was overlooking something: innovation. In particular, Simon expected that innovation would happen *because* of market signals like rising prices. If tungsten became more scarce, it would become more valuable. But the process would not end there. If tungsten were more valuable, it would make business sense for miners to go looking for more of it. It could be profitable to invent better mining technology. If neither of these work, it could be worthwhile to invent new products altogether, which meet the same needs without using tungsten at all. More people can conceive more inventions. Simon bet that, once all this innovating happened, prices would wind up going down, rather than rising.

Ten years later, Simon won his bet. The price of all five metals had fallen. Ehrlich wrote a check.

Nobody will be surprised to learn that the debate continues. Economists on both sides have suggested that if only it were a slightly different time period, or a different set of commodities, things could have been different. But mortality rates are down, not up; famines have become rarer, not more common; and England still exists. It appears that the world survived the population bomb, so far.

∾

David Lam told that story in his presidential address to the Population Association of America. In the 1960s, when Ehrlich was writing his book, the worldwide population was growing at 2 per cent a year. At that growth rate, the number of people alive would double every thirty-five years.

Population growth had never been so fast before – and it has never been so fast since. Today, the population is growing about half as fast as it was in the 1960s: at these rates, it would take seventy years to double. But that doubling almost certainly will not happen. Growth rates are still falling. Population growth is expected to head towards zero, worldwide. The best demographic projections are that the world's population will peak a little after the year 2100 with around 12 billion people.

The middle of the 20th century turns out to have been an exceptional time. The 1960s were unusual because they were a turning point in the Great Escape. Improvements in medicine, sanitation, and nutrition had started to pull down the probability that children died at the beginning of life. But fertility rates were still about as high as they had been before. As a result, not only were many babies being born, but now a larger fraction of them were also surviving. The result was rapid population growth.

Then, fertility rates started falling, too. When more of a woman's children survive, she does not need to have so many babies to ensure that some of them will survive to take care of her in old age. When economic development makes education more valuable, families have a reason to concentrate their resources on providing a better education to fewer children. Eventually, these incentives become codified in social norms: mothers-in-law and aunts come to expect the next generation of women to have fewer births than they did. Soon, mothers have about as few surviving children as they did before the Great Escape, or even fewer.

When David Lam told this story, he was speaking as an economist to a room full of demographers, sociologists, and researchers from across the social sciences. Economists love this story because it shows that people's own choices about their lives can produce an outcome that is good for everybody. Individual women each had an incentive to reduce fertility, once mortality rates started falling.

So, on average, women did. Population growth slowed. In the meantime, new technologies and institutions were invented, in response to the different demands of a larger population. The result was a population bomb that never exploded: a world with more people in it who were healthier, richer and better educated than the people in the smaller world that came before.

Will the same Escape work twice?

The analogy between population growth and ambient particles is not perfect: children are not pollution. Still, the Ehrlich–Simon bet is a classic fable in environmental economics. The escape from the population bomb teaches us that economic development does not have to mean environmental disaster. Better yet, looming disasters can create their own solutions, if change pressures people to make different decisions. Many women reduced their fertility just because they thought it would be a good idea. Changing circumstances created all the incentive that they needed to change their behaviour.

Should we expect the same rescue from air pollution? If the population bomb defused itself, perhaps we can hope that today's environmental challenges will do the same. If so, economic development would not be the cause of environmental destruction, but rather the solution.

Unfortunately, what worked for fertility reduction seems unlikely to work for air pollution or for climate change. The reason is that the incentives are different. The fertility decline of the last few decades did not happen because women and families were trying to save the earth. They happened for reasons that made sense *for that family*: more women started working in the paid labour market, education became more valuable (making children more expensive), more babies survived to be children.

These are what economists call *private* incentives, meaning that the benefits and costs are for the family or woman who makes the decision. We could imagine science fiction creatures, otherwise like humans who reproduce differently. Maybe their children are born quickly, painlessly, and immediately ready to function as (educated) adults. Some animals reproduce like that. If humans did, maybe the incentives of the late 20th century would not have made high fertility costly, and so would not have led mothers to reduce their fertility. Compared to these imaginary human-like creatures, humanity got lucky (if mothers in labour did not).

Air pollution (and, for that matter, climate change) is happening because private incentives do not match the consequences for everybody else. As we saw in Chapters 1 and 2, economists call such a mismatch an externality, because the bad consequences are external to the decision maker. Externalities are the classic case where markets left alone get things wrong.

Having a child is a decision with externalities. The rest of us will share the world with the child who you create. In many ways, that is a good thing – your child may write a song that everyone will enjoy – even if the world becomes a more crowded place by one.

The point is that having a child also has serious *private* consequences for the family who decides to have the child. Those private consequences – and not the externalities – are what defused the population bomb. Unlike high fertility, air pollution only has negative *externalities*, without the private incentives. The very reason air pollution is such a problem is that polluters lack the feedback mechanisms that will cause polluters to change their decisions. Air pollution will not defuse itself in the way the population bomb did.

Human deprivation despite economic development

India is richer, healthier, and better electrified than ever before. Many urban Indians now have large emissions footprints. And yet, much deprivation remains, especially in the non-monetary dimensions of health and well-being.

One-fifth of the world's births are in India, but one-quarter of the world's neonatal deaths occur in India. The average child in India is much shorter than would be healthy. Much stunting remains. Many women in India are underweight at the beginning of pregnancy, and gain too little weight for the growing baby's health. Do these challenges, and more, mean that India still faces too many other struggles for pollution to be a priority?

One response is the response of Chapters 1 and 2: the health and intergenerational externalities caused by air pollution mean that it is economically inefficient *not* to tackle air pollution. Economists' models are clear on this point. In a poor country, where children's health is more precarious to begin with, such externalities may be even more important.

Another response is to take India's remaining human development challenges seriously – by understanding their causes. In many cases, human development in India lags *despite* economic progress, not because of economic deprivation. This is visible in international comparisons and in differences among Indians. Unfortunately, there are many examples.

One example is child height. Children in India are shorter, on average, than children in sub-Saharan Africa. At the same level of economic wealth or poverty, children in West Bengal are shorter than children in Bangladesh. These differences are a result of differences in early-life environments. They reflect social forces and social inequality.

Open defecation is rare in Bangladesh and is uncommon in many sub-Saharan African countries. Still, it persists in India because of the continuing legacy of casteism and untouchability (Diane Coffey and I wrote about the details in our book about sanitation, *Where India Goes*). The resulting disease stunts children.

The low social status of young women is another example. Mothers in India are more likely to start pregnancy underweight than in other countries. Then, they gain too little weight during pregnancy. Mothers pass on this deprivation to their children in the form of high neonatal mortality rates: children in India are more likely than in poorer countries to die in their first month of life.

Patterns of social inequality predict child outcomes according to family rank within joint households in rural India, between different caste categories and across religions. Muslim babies are more likely to survive childhood in India than Hindu babies, even though Muslim families are poorer, on average. Again, the explanation is social: they tend to have Muslim neighbours, who turn out to be more likely to use toilets than defecate in the open, on average.

Such patterns arise again and again in the statistics of child health in India. In a dozen different ways, they explain the fundamental paradox of Indian demography: that economic development does not translate into better population health here, and that India suffers relative to poorer populations. Across a range of important cases, money simply is not the problem for Indian children's health and development: the deprivation of mothers, an environment of disease, and the pervasiveness of hierarchy are.

None of these problems has been solved by rapid economic growth. The Great Escape has ameliorated, but not eliminated,

India's social inequalities. So, these problems are unlikely to disappear merely because India becomes a little richer or better electrified. The consequence is that, although human development and the poor health of India's children rightly issue a call to action, they are not a reason to pollute in the name of economic development. Such a misdiagnosis could spread more disease while ignoring urgent challenges.

Can India afford clean air, after all?

So, can India afford to care about its air pollution? Electrification and the other benefits of modern energy transform the lives of the poor. That is important. But most Indians are not as poor as when poverty was first pitted against pollution in policy debates. Moreover, many of the deepest human development challenges that remain in India are rooted more in social inequality than in economic poverty. The upshot is that the needs to eliminate open defecation, reduce neonatal mortality, or improve child growth give no economic reason not to fight air pollution.

After decades of economic growth, there are now many Indians who could afford to sacrifice a little, if their sacrifice improved the health and human capital of everyone. The middle class becomes larger and larger every year – although most families have not yet reached it. The economics of intergenerational externalities tells us that the right sacrifice – if it were concentrated among those who can afford it, and if it reduced babies' exposure to air pollution – could lastingly increase the generation-to-generation pace of improvement.

This chapter has asked an old question: can India afford environmentalism, when electrification is so important, especially to the poor? We have considered three responses. First, India is not as poor as it used to be. In particular, many more people now have electricity. Second, the fable of the population bomb tells us that it is easy to misunderstand the apparent conflict between economics and the environment – especially because environmental pressures create economic incentives for change and innovation. Unfortunately, the self-correcting features of population change are not available to address the externalities of air pollution, so we cannot sit back and wait for the economy to do the job. (Of course, this need does not imply that actual governance is up to the task now, either.) Finally, many of India's enduring challenges to health and human development are because of social forces, not poverty. So, more electricity and more factories will not solve these important problems soon.

One further response is to ask whether poverty and economic inequality really are to blame for India's unequal distribution of electricity. The rest of this chapter follows this question to an obvious point that is often overlooked: although labelled 'economic development', access to electricity and energy in India is *already* political, depending on state choices at least as much as market forces. The implication is that different state choices would be, in principle, feasible, and that the government could distribute electricity more equitably (although I suspect that neither you nor I have a magic political wand). There is no inevitable law of engineering or economics to prevent making different decisions about electricity, to reduce both pollution and inequality. The allocation of electrical power depends on the allocation of political power.

Power cuts are not a natural phenomenon

In 2012, on the day that Sitapur voted in the Uttar Pradesh state election, I visited Lucknow for a meeting. The Sitapur bus stand is a few kilometres from where Diane and I lived, outside the town. Usually you can find something to ride most of the way from the town to our house. That night, many vehicles had been pressed into election service. The police were blocking the roads. So, along with everybody else getting down from the buses, I walked.

The bus did not reach Sitapur city until after nightfall. But, for the dozens of us walking out of town, our walk was illuminated most of the way. Hundreds of tubelights had been temporarily installed, lining the road from Sitapur out to Sudhamapuri. We all trudged home under the bright, unnatural light, while the excitement of the election buzzed around us.

A friend of mine, affiliated with the then Opposition party, stopped his car to say hello. Although not occupying any official office, he was a big enough personality in Sitapur to be allowed to drive on the dirt road belonging to the military police, even on election night. The voting was going well, he assured me. They had caught a person casting his vote twice but – not to worry – the cheater had received a thorough beating.

The illumination of the night sky on election night was as predictable as any eclipse or comet. But it was not a natural phenomenon: it was predictable if you knew the calendar of the election. Temporary outdoor tubelights mark celebrations, especially weddings. They also appear around elections to remind the voters of the electricity and other benefits that the party in power has brought to them.

When I first moved to Sitapur, I now recall with a little embarrassment, I vaguely believed that power cuts were some sort of random natural occurrence. They just *happened*, I imagined, outside of human agency. I thought this even though I gathered that they 'just happen' according to a regular schedule.

In fact, someone, somewhere, was flipping switches all along. Someone decided which neighbourhoods received electricity when. That someone had a government job. Presumably, just like the campaigners who set up tubelights on election night, that someone was therefore responding to government incentives.

∽

If electrical lights respond to the political calendar on election nights, might they do so at other times, too? Brian Min, a political science professor at the University of Michigan, suspected so. If politicians have the distribution of electricity under their control, Min realized, they could use it to try to win elections. And if politicians can use something to try to win elections, he reasoned, then they probably do so.

Min wanted to test his hypothesis, but he ran into the same problem that has blocked researchers throughout this book: data on electricity supply is not available. The government does not record, or would not share, the facts about who gets what and when. Min needed a way to see who got electricity on which days, so that he could compare before and after the election, in politically favoured and disfavoured places.

Faced with a similar problem, my co-author Sagnik measured air pollution with pictures taken by satellites. Satellites can also record anything else that is visible from space. Electricity is not visible from space, but electric lights are – at least at night. Min and other researchers have figured out that light visible from space at night can be a measure of a region's economic development. If a dark region in Bihar becomes brighter at night, especially in cities or along roads, then those lights are statistical evidence of increasing economic activity. Some economists have even started using 'night lights' measured from satellites as an alternative to GDP statistics, especially in countries without reliable national data systems.

Min was not exactly trying to use night lights as substitutes for economic statistics: he was simply interested in the electric lights themselves. Whose lights shined during political campaigns? Whose electricity came once the election was over, and whose houses stayed dark?

In the Uttar Pradesh state elections of 2002, Mayawati of the Bahujan Samaj Party (BSP) was elected to her third term as chief minister. Although she was only in office for a little more than a year, electricity moves fast. Min's data let him see the same districts at different points in time before and after the election, so he could watch night lights swell or dim.

Districts that newly voted for the BSP became brighter after the election, a signal that they received more electricity. Villages that were unlit in 2001 and switched in the 2002 election from voting for the BJP to voting for the BSP were twice as likely to become electrified by 2003 as villages that continued to support the BJP. Districts that voted for the losing party became darker. Electricity, Min concludes, was given to reward – or punish – political support.

Accustomed to living without power

Political influence over electrical power is so big that it is visible from space. One lesson from Brian Min's research is that politicians find ways to use whatever they have at hand to win elections. That is important, but not surprising. The relevant lesson for sustainable development is that 'who gets electricity' has been a political decision all along.

Observers who claim that economic progress is opposed to environmental health sometimes emphasize that poor people, in particular, are likely to not receive electricity. But if whose lights shine is a political decision, then there is no insurmountable *engineering* reason that it has to be the poor who are left out, especially in an ever-developing country. If poor people lack electrical power, it is because they lack political power. For anyone who supports both cleaner air and better lives for the poor, perhaps this fact is the place to start.

Navroz Dubash, Sunila Kale and Ranjit Bharvirkar, in their 2018 book *Mapping Power*, have catalogued the ways in which politics shapes and limits electricity delivery across India's states. In contrast with Min, Dubash and his co-authors do not interpret the voters' demands for electricity to have been a widespread engine for more and better electrification. Sometimes, they write, this does happen, such as Bihar under Nitish Kumar, or West Bengal in 2011 to 2016. But promising electricity is politically risky for state politicians: good electricity can be hard to deliver. If you succeed, voters may merely come to expect even more.

If elections do not always motivate electricity *supply*, voters instead look for electricity *subsidies*. Subsidies can take the explicit form of reduced tariffs or the implicit form of a blind eye turned to electricity theft. As a result, distribution networks cannot be reliably managed; electricity demand cannot be controlled; and funds are not available to invest in better systems. (The MD of the Kanpur distribution company is nodding along from her wooden conference room.)

Of course, Dubash's collaborators realize that state politics is unlikely to eliminate subsidies any time soon. The Samajwadi Party MLA from Kanpur agrees with that part. Reforming financing mechanisms and investing in distribution networks, they conclude, could energize development for nearer-term years, while easing the longer-term transition to renewable sources. Are such changes likely? The answer depends on the political interests that state leaders perceive, or can construct for themselves.

～

I once had a chance to discuss the intentional allocation of electricity with the man who was then general manager (GM) of the Kanpur coal plant. He invited me in for a cup of tea. Like in other bureaucratic offices, the administrator sat behind a large glass-covered desk and in front of a list of every GM since 1973.

His particular job was to oversee electricity production, not distribution. An electronic board behind the rows of chairs monitored the plant's productivity. In principle, it could produce 220 MW, but that day each of two generators was producing about 70 MW, for a total of 140 MW. The plant is small and had become old, the GM explained.

The implication, the GM told me, is that there is not enough electricity for everybody. Even in Kanpur city, there are six hours of power cuts every day. To the GM, it was clear that electricity should go to the urbanites first. His assistant elaborated: 'When we have extra power we give it to the people in the remote villages. They don't need it; they are accustomed to living without it.'

Meanwhile, outside the coal plant, the corporate offices were separated from the plant by a dense forest of electrical wires. The government's wires thinned out as they stretched from the power plant, over the accustomed poor people's houses nearby, towards richer neighbourhoods beyond and on to somewhere else.

5

Heat and Humidity

In 2016, Churu district of Rajasthan attained fame twice. First, it became one of the first districts in India to proclaim itself free from open defecation, under the prime minister's sanitation drive. Second, in the heat of the summer, its temperature crossed 50°C. Churu's peak was just under Phalodi's, which set the record of 51°C at about the same time. Nikhil and I wondered what to make of the sanitation claims. Meanwhile, we suspected that such high temperatures would have had serious consequences on people's health. So, we made our way to Churu to find out.

Although Rajasthan's hot summer was record-setting, there is nothing exceptional any more about exceptional temperatures. New temperature records are being set all around the world. As I write in 2018, the four hottest years on record are 2016, 2015, 2017 and 2014. Average temperatures are increasing. So are temperature peaks. In 1972, the year of Indira Gandhi's speech in Sweden, there were 197 days above 32°C in Kanpur. By 2017, there were 227 such warm days there. By 2052, models project anywhere from 233 to 251 days. Whatever the consequences of heat may be, India is experiencing more and more hot days.

Nikhil and I did not find these consequences in Churu. It was the rare trip to villages where we did not learn very much at all. Churu was not open-defecation free. On the first day, a shopkeeper asked whether, in exchange for our nosy questions about toilets, we wanted the real answer or the official answer. Our impressions about the real answer were verified when data from a March 2016 survey showed that 19 per cent of rural households in Churu still defecated in the open.

After settling toilets, we turned to temperature. Scientific research made us expect to find tales of babies or the elderly dying in the heat. Yet, nobody seemed to think it was that big of a deal. Sure, it was unpleasant to live through, but not the sort of thing you died from. People were polite to us at the district hospital; some villagers told us about the summer, and a dispensary owner wanted to talk our ears off. Still, nobody thought it was exceptional.

Where did Nikhil and I go wrong? As ever, Nikhil tried to take the blame. Just the week before, my father had been diagnosed with lung cancer. Learning that – and after enduring the Delhi air pollution experiment in Chapter 1 — Nikhil decided that he had inhaled enough cigarette smoke. He quit smoking. Cold turkey. Several times. And eventually, successfully.

Our trip to Rajasthan was part fieldwork, part detox. Day and night, I did not let Nikhil out of my sight for a week. An unfortunate side effect was a noticeable sharpening of the ordinarily smooth and comforting lines of Nikhil's interviewing technique.

Nicotine withdrawal was not to blame for our high-temperature hijinks, I eventually realized. The project of finding victims of climate change simply never made sense. Yes, high temperatures are deadly. Climate change is going to make exposure to extreme temperature an ever bigger problem for India. But, rural Rajasthanis have ways of coping with the extreme heat. For example, people living in hot places know to take shelter in the shade in the heat of the mid-day, when the only people out are Nikhil hunting for a cigarette and me chasing after him. Moreover, while the effects will add up over the large population of India and the many hot decades to come, the probability of heat killing any one child is small. And, even if we found a child who appeared to die from the heat, it would be difficult to be sure that the true cause was not actually something else. Climate change's deaths are real people, but they are easier to find in statistics than in a village visit.

The upshot is that this chapter on climate policy is more abstract and more statistical than the rest of this book. Air pollution's victims are easy to find. Many children spend all winter with runny noses. Healthy young adults in Delhi get pneumonia. Even the chief minister of Delhi appears to suffer from the particles in the air. Climate change's damages are less obvious for now, in part because they are only beginning. Many Indian babies will die at the start of life unless global climate policies improve. This chapter cannot introduce you to their mothers, because neither those babies nor many of their parents are born yet.

The basic threats of climate change are settled scientific fact. Emissions of CO_2 and other greenhouse gasses are accumulating in the atmosphere. Most of these carbon emissions have been from richer countries. Much of them are from burning fuel to generate energy. The consequence will be that the earth will trap ever more heat from the sun. Global temperatures will rise on average. Extremely hot days will become more common. The only way to prevent large changes in temperature would be to limit the atmospheric concentration of greenhouse gases. But concentrations are rising fast; nobody knows exactly what temperature changes will result, and nobody knows exactly when and whether global policymakers will get serious about reducing carbon emissions.

This chapter begins to ask what India should do about it. People in India will be highly vulnerable to climate change's harms. But the country cannot prevent climate change on its own, even if it somehow could manage to stop emitting carbon altogether. India has little choice but to think critically about the best response it has available to the indefensible injustice of rich countries' carbon pollution and climate policies. The starting point is to understand what is at stake: what might climate change mean for future Indians?

Heat, humidity and mortality

On top of our other problems, Nikhil and I turned out to be hunting for climate deaths at the wrong time of the year. We were looking for deaths from the dry heat of the peak summer. But our plan overlooked some of the science about how heat kills humans. Sitting awake with Nikhil in an old haveli in Churu, I did what I always do on fieldwork nights: I read paperback murder mysteries. If this book were a murder mystery, by Chapter 5 you would be suspecting you knew the killer (hint: particles in the air). When you do, the plot twists. It is time for another death, and another killer.

In this chapter, the surprising other killer turns out to be not merely heat alone, but especially heat in combination with humidity. High humidity prevents human bodies from cooling themselves. The implication is that climate change will hit South Asians hard: sub-Saharan Africans have dry heat, but India has the monsoon. When the monsoon makes it to Churu, the weather cools off a little. But in parts of UP, Bihar and Bangladesh where humidity co-exists with short-of-record-setting heat, the weather does not become dangerous until the monsoon months. It is not May and June that are deadly there. It is July, August, and September, when the rains come. Because other countries do not have the same pattern of humidity, India is especially vulnerable to this consequence of climate change.

When our bodies digest food and our organs do their work, the energy generates heat. To stay alive, human bodies have to cool down somehow. When the temperature of the air is cooler than the temperature of our skin, this is easy: we lose our heat to the surrounding air.

When the temperature of the air is hotter than our skin, there is only one thing human bodies can do to cool off: sweat. Humans sweat because the evaporation of the water cools our bodies. As sweat turns from liquid to gas, it takes some of our heat with it. Whether sweat can evaporate depends on humidity: that is, on how much moisture is already in the air. On a day that is both very hot and very humid, human bodies have a problem. Because of the heat, we need to cool off by sweating; but because of the humidity, we cannot. Even after a few hours exposed to very high heat and humidity, even in the shade, a healthy human will die.

Globally, hours that are both sufficiently hot and sufficiently humid to be lethal are rare. Even in India, such hours are uncommon. But they are becoming more common. And climate change will bring many more. Climate change will increase the earth's average temperature by a few degrees. 'A few degrees' does not sound like much, but a slightly hotter world will shift odds that are currently manageable. Extremely hot days will change from 'rare' to 'unusual' – from, in some places, one in a thousand to one in a hundred. Because it is the extreme days that are deadly, a small increase in average temperature could lead to a large increase in danger to humans.

Nobody has experienced the future weather. But scientists are able to project how many extremely hot days there will be in the future with computer models. In these models, 'wet bulb temperature' is an important number. Wet bulb temperature is the temperature that a thermometer would show if it were wrapped in a damp cloth. Scientists invented wet bulb temperature to reflect the physics of human temperature regulation. For example, the US Navy uses wet bulb temperature to decide whether its personnel should work outside and what it is safe for them to wear. In this system, 'dry bulb temperature' is just the name for normal temperature. Wet bulb temperature is always less than dry bulb temperature, except at 100 per cent humidity. The higher the humidity, the closer wet bulb temperature is to dry bulb temperature.

Humans cannot survive more than a few hours exposed to a wet bulb temperature of 35°C. This upper limit is a simple consequence of the physics of heat. At 50 per cent humidity, 35°C wet bulb would be a dry bulb (or, normal) temperature of 40°C. You may have experienced many hours of temperature above 40°C, but not at such a high humidity. Hours of wet bulb temperature above 30°C are currently rare, anywhere in the world. For now, wet bulb temperature almost never goes above 31°C, anywhere.

As the climate changes, lethally hot and humid days will not be so rare any more. Stephen Sherwood and Matthew Huber are two climate scientists. They used a computer model to project how often high wet bulb temperatures would occur under a bad-case climate change scenario – the sort of outcome that is possible, but that everyone hopes climate policy will manage to avoid. Under the scenario they investigate – with 10°C of climate change – most of the land where people now live would become uninhabitable due to unsurvivable outdoor wet bulb temperatures. Essentially all of India, outside of the mountains, would sometimes experience days about 35°C wet bulb.

A follow-up research team led by Eun-Soon Im, a professor in Hong Kong, focused on South Asia. They studied an 8.5°C scenario: very bad, but less extreme. Their computations found that northern plains cities like Lucknow and Patna would begin to have lethal days above 35°C within the 21st century. Even under 'only' 4.5°C of change, the authors conclude, 'vast regions of South Asia are projected to experience episodes exceeding 31°C [wet bulb], which is considered extremely dangerous for most humans'.

The outdoors might become – literally, if episodically – unsurvivable. This possibility is both disturbing and real. To emphasize: scientists know this because of computer models based on physics, not because anybody has seen it yet. There is no reason to doubt the math of the models, but they can only tell us about physics. That means that some of the most important questions are wide open. We have no way to know how human societies, governments and markets will rearrange if (when?) part of South Asia's currently urbanized surface becomes seasonally lethal.

There is another important question that physics' theoretical upper limit does not answer. What happens as we get close to the limit? How bad is exposure to wet bulb temperatures that are anomalously high, but short of 35°C?

The bad news is that such hot days already happen and are becoming ever more common. The good news is that, if they exist, we can measure and study them. For years, Mike Geruso and I have collaborated to study the economics of population health. When I decided to work on environmental economics, I sent Mike the computer-model paper about deadly wet bulb temperatures. We realized that we could learn about the effects of high, but not surpassingly high temperatures by studying the variation in the weather that already exists.

Many population health scientists have already written many statistical papers about the deadly consequences of high (ordinary, dry bulb) temperatures. More people die – and especially more older adults die – during spells of very high temperature. High temperatures put stress on the body. Our hearts and circulatory systems have to work harder to bring heat from our interiors to our skin, where we can lose the heat to the environment. If that work becomes too hard, it might fail, particularly in a body already weakened by old age, deprivation or disease.

To study the statistics of mortality, deaths must be recorded somewhere. We faced this problem before in Chapter 1. Because India does not register all births and deaths, there is little hope of detecting the effect of air pollution on mortality. Studying temperature in developing countries has the same problem. Almost all the existing research about temperature and mortality investigates deaths in the developed world – especially in the US. But Mike and I expected the consequences to be much worse in poorer populations. In developing countries, families are poorer, health is weaker, clinics have fewer resources, and homes and buildings only partially separate the indoors from out. Recall Manju's triplets, whose mud house had no door. So, researchers could have missed the most important risks, because of their reasonable strategy of looking where the data is.

In Chapter 1, the fact that India does not register its deaths was the end of the road for learning whether its air pollution kills children. But, to study temperature, we have a backup option that is not available for pollution. No country has as many particles in the air as India, so no other population's data is a substitute. But other countries do have extreme temperatures. Of course, other developing countries also do not have birth and death registries: India is no exception there. But many countries do have sample surveys.

For the past few decades, the Demographic and Health Surveys have collected comparable data on births and deaths from around the world. Every few years, within many countries, a representative sample of mothers is asked about each time they have given birth and about the baby. The resulting body of information is one of humanity's treasures. It is one of the only ways we know how patterns of birth and death are changing in the vast populations without vital registration systems. Because these are sample surveys, no one dataset would be large enough to detect smallish effects of rare hot days. Luckily, the survey has happened over a hundred times.

Over two years, Mike and I – and especially Melissa LoPalo, a fellow economist from Texas who joined our team – assembled every useable survey that existed. Melissa wrangled the University of Texas's supercomputer to compress enormous records of global weather into a summary of what each baby, from over fifty developing countries, was exposed to in its month of birth. In the end, we had statistics on several million births – ten times more than the data on height in Chapter 1.

Although most other researchers had studied the effect of temperature on older adults, we looked for an effect on the youngest babies. Before a baby is born, it does not need to control its own temperature. Its mother's body does that work. In the days or first few weeks after birth, babies are still developing the ability to regulate their temperature and to sweat. In fact, much of what is important about neonatal care is managing babies' temperature. In almost every case, the problem is that babies are too *cold*. One of the most life-saving healthcare techniques, called 'kangaroo mother care', is as simple as clasping an undressed neonate right up against a new mother's bare chest:

the mother keeps the baby warm, and the baby is encouraged to begin eating.

First breaths and last breaths

Mike, Melissa and I were interested in the rare case when a baby is born into an environment that is so hot and humid as to have the opposite problem. Babies have little control over their bodies, physiologically and socially. They cannot complain specifically about the temperature, or move themselves to a more comfortable place. Papers by biologists about early-life body temperature told us to suspect an effect of heat and humidity on death at the beginning of life. Only with our enormous assembled dataset could we look for it.

Exposure to the combination of high heat and humidity kills neonates, we found. If 100 babies are exposed to a full week of very high wet bulb temperature in the month they are born, about one more of them (a little less, in fact), would be expected to die, on average. Several days of such an extreme combination would currently be a very rare event. So, this effect is not a large factor in the neonatal mortality that occurs today in India. But its importance is growing: days with high wet bulb temperature are already becoming more common.

Our large collection of surveys lets us double-check that the extra neonatal deaths we found are because of the weather – and not just a coincidence. For example, one worry is that healthier mothers might turn out to have their babies at different times of the year than less healthy mothers, on average. If it is unpleasant to be in the third trimester of pregnancy in May, for example, better-educated mothers might be less likely to give birth in July.

In our survey data, mothers are asked about all their births, whenever they happened. So, in the same village, we see babies born in the same month of different years: July 2014, for example, July 2012, and July 2011. As a result, we can compare babies born in the same calendar month, in the same village: all in July in Chhotagaon, for example, but in different years. This strategy accounts for any *predictable* aspect of seasonality and the annual calendar; it only draws conclusions from the unpredictable part. The predictable part is the only part that mothers and families know about when they are deciding whether or not to get pregnant. They do not know, nine months in advance, how the *actual* weather in the month they give birth will turn out to be different from an *average* month of that type, in that place.

We found the same effect of hot, humid days on babies' survival whether or not we restricted our comparison to babies born in different years of the same place and month. That fact is good evidence that we indeed found a credible problem. In a similar double-check, we repeated our data analysis, but substituted weather in the same month and place one year after the actual year and month when the baby was born. This intentionally mistimed data would follow many similar patterns as the correctly timed data, but could not actually reflect a real effect on neonatal death. There is no way that weather a year after you are born could reach back in time and kill you. So, we hoped not to find an 'effect' – and we did not. In short, all of these statistical tools suggest that the deadly consequences of heat and humidity are real.

In the year 2100, by the time climate change is well under way, the effect of hot weather on infant death will, hopefully, not be as large as it is today. Air conditioning protects from both heat and humidity. Most babies in rich countries are born in climate-controlled, indoor environments. They hardly go outside in their first month of life. Eventually, as economic development continues, that will be true in India too. (Maybe air conditioning will become less energy intensive.)

For now, the maternity ward of the Kanpur district hospital is exposed to the outside air. Nothing keeps the air in the inner rooms of the hospital from being any different from the air outside: no less polluted, no less humid. Large parts of the walls are open, or partially covered with metal grates. When I visited in a statistically deadly July, ceiling fans were not turning and coolers were not operating in the emergency room for males (I did not enter the females' ward). Around the perimeter of the building are various defunct or silent coolers. One big entrance hall had the largest metal cooler box I had ever seen, not operating.

The situation was the same in the maternity ward – except that, being upstairs, it was even hotter. Here, too, nothing prevented the babies' first breath of air from matching the air outside. Some windows were half-covered with opaque green plastic to protect the mothers' modesty, but nothing would prevent air from passing through. Six very high ceiling fans turned lazily in the large room, far above the women and their babies. These were the babies privileged enough to be born in a top medical facility in the city.

India's climate vulnerability

Most people already know that climate change is an approaching disaster. Still, learning that heat and humidity together kill neonates prompts us to update our worries in two ways. First, evidence already pointed to an effect of high temperatures on mortality, but these deaths were deaths among the oldest adults. Every preventable death is tragedy, but when a baby dies, many more years of life are lost. Moreover, a population with many infant deaths is usually a population where families choose to have more children. Higher fertility has consequences for women's freedom and for the whole economy.

Second, our data is clear that neonates are killed by temperature *and* humidity, not merely temperature alone. The implication is that these deaths will happen in South Asia and other hot and humid places. Many people think of sub-Saharan Africa or small island countries when they picture the populations most vulnerable to climate change. But heat in sub-Saharan Africa, even where temperatures are hotter than India's, is generally dry heat. In dry heat, sweat can do its job. Because heat is even more deadly with humidity, future Indians will be especially likely to suffer this particular threat.

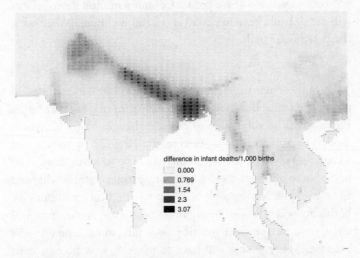

difference in infant deaths/1,000 births

0.000
0.769
1.54
2.3
3.07

Figure 10. Additional infant deaths that are projected to happen in India in 2050 under a worse climate change scenario, relative to a better climate change scenario.

Figure 10 shows what is at stake for India in climate policy. The figure plots the difference between two alternative policy futures: one in which little is done to control carbon emissions and climate change, and one in which the policy to reduce greenhouse gas emissions fast becomes aggressive. The projection is based on the effect of wet bulb temperature that Mike, Melissa and I found. Many more babies will die in India if carbon emissions are not controlled. These deaths are concentrated in states that are already disadvantaged. Political consequences could magnify the harms of climate change, if damages turn out to increase inequality.

Worse still, 2050 is near-term for climate change. Effects may only get worse in the decades and centuries to come. Combining the projection in Figure 10 with population projections yields a grave product: about a million more infants will die in India between 2050 and 2100 if climate policy takes the pessimistic path.

∾

The deadly effects of heat and humidity will be concentrated in places like India. But mortality is hardly the only way that future Indians will be vulnerable to climate change. Many economic models document large costs of rearranging society to adapt to a changing climate. Infrastructure will have to move, change, or both. Some investments will become worthless; others will need to be re-done. Most people will survive the heat and humidity, but many will fall ill in newly important ways. Agriculture will change: some standard practices will fail, some expenses will increase. Many people will have to move to new homes, learn new ways of life – cope with changes that make their lives worse than they could have been.

One economic consequence is that, in the heat and humidity, humans will not be able to work as hard outdoors. After Melissa had assembled the combined data to study infant deaths, she realized that she had a tool for many purposes. She turned her attention to the interviewers: the survey employees who collect the interviews, moving from house to hut to farm outside. Economists had been looking for an opportunity to estimate the effect of extreme heat on labour productivity. Because survey data is collected by workers, Melissa found one.

On hot and humid days, she found, surveyors work less productively. In any given hour, they get less quality work done. In part, they compensate by working more hours for the same pay, enjoying less free time. Melissa interviewed surveyors and found the paperwork that their supervisors use to track their productivity. Surveyors know that it is easier for their supervisors to *count* completed surveys than to monitor the *quality* of their work. She showed that one strategic way that interviewers cope with hot days is by working more hours, but with more mistakes. Most outdoor workers are not demographic surveyors, of course. But as long as humans work outside, effects of the weather on our productivity will matter for economic outcomes.

A recent World Bank report offered one attempt at adding up all the likely costs of climate change for India's future economy. The leading author is Muthukumara Mani. When he presented his findings to an overflowing audience at the Habitat Centre in Delhi, Mani was careful to emphasize that any economic model of such an uncertain future must make its best guesses from the available information. We cannot ignore climate change: our only option is to make the wisest policy possible with the alarming evidence that is available.

Mani's numbers were indeed alarming. The World Bank is naturally interested in economic implications: 'Translated into gross domestic product (GDP) per capita, changes in average weather are predicted to reduce income in severe hotspots by 14.4 per cent in Bangladesh, 9.8 per cent in India, and 10.0 per cent in Sri Lanka by 2050 under the carbon-intensive scenario compared to the climate of today.' Of course, India would make up a 10 per cent loss to GDP after a couple of years of economic growth, if the recent fast pace continues. But some people would lose much more than others. What is more striking about that conclusion is that 2050 is so soon – most of climate change's damages will only be initially unfolding by 2050, with the worst yet to come.

Worse still, India's 'severe hotspots' are likely to be found in the northern plains states that are already poor. Similarly, the highly hot and humid days that threaten neonates are expected to be most common in and around Uttar Pradesh and Bihar. The harms from climate change are going to increase inequality within India, by hurting regions that are already disadvantaged. No World Bank model can predict all the political consequences of an economic slowdown that promotes inequality and large-scale migration.

Climate vulnerability is not an international contest. Future sub-Saharan Africans will be vulnerable to some dimensions of climate change; small island countries to others. The point is that India is right up the list. Understandably, when decades of Indian policymakers have considered environmental policy, they have emphasized a need for the sort of economic development that would eventually upgrade the facilities at the Kanpur hospital's maternity ward. Climate change requires a more complicated account of India's national interests. Future Indians are in the front ranks of the world's climate-vulnerable populations.

Should India save itself?

What should India do about its deep climate vulnerability? One natural reaction is to wonder if India should save itself. Should India eliminate its own carbon emissions? Climate change is a global problem, but perhaps India's climate vulnerability is a good reason to decarbonize unilaterally.

The emissions policies of the developed world are appalling. So, decades of India's leaders expressing justified outrage are understandable. And yet, this policy has not been effective at changing the behaviour of the likes of Donald Trump. The stakes are too high for India to continue a hortatory strategy that is doomed to fail. But what should India do? Should it try to save itself by transitioning to carbon-free energy? Such a reorganization would be costly. But would it be worth it?

If democratic India is going to solve the problem by eliminating its own emissions, one starting question is whether Indian citizens would be willing to sacrifice to avoid climate change. At r.i.c.e., I am lucky enough to work with a plucky team that hunts out the data it needs to answer the questions at hand. A few years ago, Diane, our colleague Payal Hathi, and Amit Thorat, a professor at Jawaharlal Nehru University, realized that debates about prejudice had grown predictable and stale. Some citizens, concerned about social inequality, emphasize proof that discrimination continues. Others point to the fact that disadvantaged groups are not as badly off as they used to be. Meanwhile, privileged elites defensively assert that they themselves are certainly not prejudiced against other religions or castes. (So what is the fuss about?)

Diane, Payal and Amit hoped that statistically tracking social attitudes over time could move the conversation beyond anecdotes, while following whatever progress occurs. The data did not yet exist, but that was a mere practical problem. They established their own call centre and developed techniques for representative mobile phone surveys in India. The hard part was developing sampling techniques to ensure that survey respondents would be representative of everyone. Surveyors make sure to talk to randomly selected adults – not only to whoever happens to have a phone. The result was a new survey called Social Attitudes Research, India (SARI).

In the second round of the survey, Amit and Diane offered me the chance to add a survey question on climate change. We were interested in what the public at large thought and whether they would be willing to contribute to averting disasters. From August 2016 to May 2017, surveyors interviewed over 4,000 respondents in two samples, one representative of adults in Rajasthan, and another representative of men in Mumbai. The interviewers posed one of several versions of a question:

'Now I will talk about a problem that your grandchildren might have to face. Many scientists believe that the earth will become very warm, to an extent that agriculture will become difficult and people will start falling sick. One of the reasons could be that the way electricity is produced today creates a lot of heat. This is making the earth warmer. Some scientists feel that one solution to this problem could be to cut down the use of electricity which may reduce rising temperatures in the future.

'Would you be willing to bear an additional three hours of electricity cuts so that the temperature does not rise more by the time your grandchildren are living?'

Not every respondent was asked about three hours. The survey had a randomized experiment built in. So, one-third of participants were asked if they would accept one more hour of cut, and one-third were asked if they would accept five hours.

Overall, about three-fourths of participants said that they would accept electricity cuts to prevent climate change. The 'price' of the sacrifice mattered. More than 80 per cent were willing to accept one hour of cut; about two-thirds would accept five hours. We were glad to see that the answer depended on the number of hours – it confirmed that respondents were paying some attention to the question! When we split the sample into men or women, Mumbai or Rajasthan, the numbers did not change much further. Taken together, we found that citizens, on average, were willing to contribute to escaping disaster.

What do these results mean? It is heartening to know that many Rajasthanis would be willing to give up some of the little electricity they have, if they could protect their descendants from climate change. But this fact hardly settles the questions of climate policy. For one, any proposal that the rural poor should be the first to sacrifice is ethically outrageous. For another, the question was *hypothetical*: in actual fact, most people in Rajasthan are responsible for few CO_2 emissions. Rajasthanis therefore have little sacrifice to offer. This reality suggests a question: *are* there people in India who are responsible for enough emissions that they should face a cut?

India's own high emitters

Two people within the same country can have different carbon footprints. A 2010 study in *Proceedings of the National Academy of Sciences* counted over a billion people around the world who emit more CO_2 than a reasonable international cap would permit. Shoibal Chakravarty and his co-authors imagined a global target of 30 gigatons of CO_2 emissions in 2030. This limit would cap each person at 10.8 tons per year. Shoibal's team matched data on each country's emissions to facts about the distribution of income within a country. From this, they computed how many people are economically responsible for more emissions than the cap permits – more than 10.8 tons per year.

For the US, Chakravarty's team projected that most people would be unsustainably high emitters in 2030. Almost 80 per cent of Americans and Canadians would be emitting more than their fair share. About 300 million people in China would also be responsible for too-high emissions. But buried deep in the online supplementary appendix to the paper, the authors compute that, even in 2030, almost nobody in India would count among the high emitters. This is surprising. India's economy is growing quickly and will probably continue to grow over the next decade. India is poorer than China, but not so much poorer. Some people in India are very rich: flying in planes and driving in cars. What about their emissions?

I reached out to Shoibal Chakravarty to ask about the computations for India. Shoibal explained that detailed information on income inequality for each country was very difficult to find. So, their team had to settle on rough databases that split the population into five bins: the poorest 20 per cent, the richest 20 per cent, and the three groups in the middle. For some small countries, the five groups concept captures the basic facts about inequality. But India is too large for five groups. 'The top 20 per cent' of India itself contains much inequality: in 2030, this group will be almost as populous as the US was when Chakravarty's paper was written in 2010. So, this strategy was bound to miss the economic elite of India, hidden within the top 20 per cent.

Shoibal agreed. So, we worked together to update the numbers. Instead of five groups, we used the entire distribution of rich and poor found in the 2012 India Human Development Survey. This allowed us to capture the inequality at the top. The result was that we found many more high emitters in India. In 2030, India would have about as many as would be in Mexico, or in Australia and New Zealand combined, or almost as many as in Canada.

Of course, this number would still be a small fraction of India's overall population, but it means that India would have a population of high emitters as large as many rich countries do. If you think that what matters ethically is what *people* do – and is not arbitrary international boundaries that were drawn by colonialists' violence – then it is difficult to escape the conclusion that high emitters who happen to live in India are among the many people worldwide who should cut back.

Moreover, the survey data lets us see who within India would be responsible for high emissions. Because economic inequality is correlated with social inequality, emissions responsibility is similarly correlated. Familiar categories of advantage and disadvantage predict who turns out to be included among the high emitters. Over 3 per cent of Brahmins are projected each to be responsible for more than 10.8 tons of emissions in 2030, compared with less than half of 1 per cent of Dalits.

Be the change you want to see?

So, should India respond to its climate vulnerability by eliminating its own emissions? We have seen that many Indians are willing to sacrifice to avoid climate change. And millions – or tens of millions – will soon be responsible for more emissions than their global fair share. But the question that we have ignored so far is perhaps the most important: would it do any good?

India's emissions are currently low, as part of the global total. Sophisticated models are not needed to conclude that they are almost insignificant compared to richer economies' carbon footprints. But what matters is the total stock of emissions, added up over the present, past and future. On all accounts, India's emissions are going to continue expanding over the coming decades. So, any benefit of India decarbonising would not happen because of today's pollution. The benefit would be the many future decades of possibly large emissions that turn out not to happen.

Could India eliminate its climate vulnerability by turning off that entire future trajectory of emissions? Computer models of the climate and the economy are used to evaluate possible environmental policies. I was part of a research team (along with a macroeconomist and a climate-policy modeller) who asked what would happen if India alone stopped industrial emissions – and left the rest of the world to do what it would otherwise do.

Not much, the computer told us. If every country, including India, pursues business as usual without important emissions reductions, then climate change is likely to be huge: slightly more than 6°C. If, instead, India acts alone, eliminating all of its present and future emissions, climate change would be… slightly less than 6°C. (Different model assumptions would yield a different number than 6°C: the point is that India alone makes little difference between the two.) In fact, the improvement would probably be even smaller than the model projects, because it is not programmed to consider the fact that other countries' economies would step in to produce the products that a decarbonized India would not.

This chapter contains little good news. Perhaps this is the worst of it. Climate policy, at its core, is an international problem. India is deeply vulnerable and is already suffering from the emissions of the developed world. Yet, even if it were willing to sacrifice more than anyone could recommend, India could not save itself alone.

If India escapes the worst of climate change, it will be because other countries change course. So, the important question is how India can influence that change. When we computed 6°C of global warming – with or without Indian emissions – our computer program did not consider the political chain reaction that might follow from the extreme example India would set by (unrealistically) eliminating emissions.

Chances are that if India decided to be the face of a changed emissions policy it wants to see in the world, it would have *some* influence on the political conversation elsewhere. Still, such hope alone is not enough to make India's unilateral complete decarbonisation a good idea yet. What about an intermediate path? To understand what India should hope for and work for in international climate coordination, we will need to move beyond India's emissions, and find a way to understand the whole world.

How to win a Nobel prize for something every economist already knows

In Chapter 2, we saw that India's air pollution is what economists call an externality. Climate change may be the greatest externality that human economies have ever yet suffered. When I take an Uber in Delhi from CR Park to the Indian Statistical Institute, the exhaust fills the air we all share. When the coal plant in Kanpur generates energy to electrify Uttar Pradesh's villages, the smoke diffuses for kilometres around. Power plants and airplane flights in the US decades ago are already warming the atmosphere into which Indian children are born today. And all of us, who are rich enough to buy a book, are participating in emissions that will change lives for future generations.

That sounds like a daunting problem for economists. But in fact, the solution is simple enough to be included in every introductory microeconomics class. The optimal response to an externality is to internalize it: make sure decision-makers have to pay the social marginal cost. The result is blackboard magic: families and businesses and everyone else would then choose the amount where the extra harm from the pollution just balances the extra benefits from the polluting activity. In other words, a carbon tax harnesses economic incentives to get climate policy right. And, with coloured chalk, it makes a beautiful blackboard diagram too.

Drawing that picture is easy. Figuring out what the number of the carbon tax should be is a harder problem. For solving that problem, William Nordhaus won a share of the 2018 Nobel

Prize in Economics. Nordhaus is an economist who has been a professor at Yale since 1967, when he earned his PhD from MIT. In the 1990s, Nordhaus built one of the first computer programs that could do it. This is a Nobel-worthy contribution, and not merely because of its importance for practical policymaking. The Obama administration and other governments used Nordhaus's software, alongside other models.

It is also worthy because of what it highlights for policy. Climate change, for all of its apparent enormity, is a problem within the reach of everyday economics. After Nobel prizes for frontier econometrics, for behavioural innovations, and for abstract theory, Nordhaus's Nobel celebrated the classic lessons at the core of public economics – and the importance of translating these lessons into practice.

∽

Nordhaus developed an 'Integrated Assessment Model', often abbreviated as an IAM. The model is 'integrated' because it combines standard equations for economic growth with a model of climate science – including our best understanding of the cumulative effect of emissions on temperature change. Then, the model wraps temperature change back to its economic and human development consequences, using an equation called the 'damage function'. The damage function translates temperature increases into lost consumption – and therefore, lost well-being.

Then, the model optimizes. It chooses a carbon tax such that the benefits of polluting economic activity balance against the costs of climate change and the damages it causes. Those benefits are important: the whole world's optimal amount of carbon emissions anywhere is not yet zero, because emission-generating economic activity has important benefits. But, alternatives to carbon-based energy are becoming ever cheaper. The world is becoming richer. As Nordhaus's model concludes, the world should be moving towards drawing down emissions, even at an economic cost.

What makes the modelling so difficult is that the people involved are many and diverse. Choosing an optimal carbon tax would have implications for urbanites and villagers in India today; for Bangladeshi children born into dangerous heat a few decades from now; for rich Americans upgrading their car; and for everyone, everywhere, a century from now. Some are helped, many are harmed, and the billions upon billions of future victims add up to a lot of 'marginal social cost'.

Nordhaus's model, like any optimising IAM, has to balance these diverse costs and benefits for rich and poor people: today, tomorrow, and in the further future. This is done, like any other optimisation problem, with an assumed goal within the model for society to pursue: a 'social welfare function' that adds up costs and benefits. Researchers building upon Nordhaus's model have shown that it matters how the social welfare function values future benefits and costs, relative to present ones. So does how it weighs how poorer people are harmed against how richer people are harmed. Still, a consensus has emerged that for a vast range of plausible social objectives, global climate policy should be aggressive now and even more aggressive soon. If not, many future people will suffer the consequences of climate change.

Nordhaus's original model, called DICE, rolled the whole world into one representative economy. IAMs have been criticized for being simple, but simplification is necessary for a model covering 300 years, complex processes, and the whole world's economic growth (all optimized using 1990s computers). Nordhaus later developed DICE into a regionally disaggregated version. India was one of the regions.

In developing a regional IAM, Nordhaus had to incorporate properties of each region. He drew these from statistical research where available. He also had to make some quantitative assumptions. Over the years, as research has progressed, successive versions of the model have refined its assumptions. Research on climate vulnerability is still ongoing. In fact, only in the past few years have economists turned their statistical tools toward understanding the effects of temperature – such as Mike and I investigating neonatal mortality.

When Nordhaus started, such estimates were not yet available. Among the lessons of the new econometrics of temperature is that climate damages may be even greater than what Nordhaus's model assumes. For example, for now, the interaction of heat and humidity is not part of Nordhaus's IAMs. Instead, damage functions reflect ordinary dry bulb temperatures. But there is no conceptual reason that an IAM could not incorporate humidity. Work towards that goal is under way. The upshot will be that India's harm from climate change will be even more severe. In the model, the social marginal cost of emissions would increase. So, mitigation policy would become an even greater priority.

Using Nordhaus's toolbox

Nordhaus's particular IAMs are far from the last word on climate policy. They are valuable because they are a toolbox that anyone can download, modify, and use to investigate their own version of Nordhaus's questions. One of Nordhaus's contributions was to put his model on the internet. You can download it too, and investigate your own version. Many Nobel prizes have been given for work that was done and over with long ago. Nordhaus's prize, for providing tools to understand climate policy, is for critical but unfinished work in progress.

A few years ago, I collaborated with a research team that noticed something odd about the assumptions in Nordhaus's regional model. The computer program assumed that 'total factor productivity' (familiar to macroeconomists as the mysterious ultimate driver of economic growth) would rapidly increase and converge towards the rich countries, even in the world's poorest economies. The history of economic development is a history of confident predictions of international economic convergence right around the corner, followed again and again by what Lant Pritchett famously called 'divergence, big time'. The model also was using population projections that missed the fact that sub-Saharan Africa's demographic transition is going slower than demographers once expected.

Anyone would hope that socioeconomic development in Africa, India, and the rest of the developing world happens quickly – but what if it does not? Then the future developing world would be poorer than Nordhaus was assuming. So, climate damages would hit an already more-disadvantaged, vulnerable population. We took Nordhaus's model, tweaked the assumptions, and computed the consequences for optimal climate policy. The result confirmed our worry that the IAM's recommendation might be too optimistic about economic development. If we can expect climate change to harm many poor people, then we should do even more to prevent it now than Nordhaus originally recommended.

The implication is that economic development and environmental sustainability are again partners to one another, rather than in conflict. Investments that accelerate human development could make future populations healthier and more resilient, reducing the damage that climate change does. Of course, these benefits only happen if investments really do translate into human development – as we saw in Chapter 4, India's background of social inequality creates special challenges. Still, human development and climate mitigation are both necessary.

Is inequality about economics or politics?

Although more studies of climate policy emerge each year, there are still facts that nobody knows. Many aspects of the future remain difficult to predict. Inequality is one of the hardest. Economists' tools are built to understand averages. 'What was the average effect of a government programme?' a microeconomic study might ask. 'What will happen to GDP per capita?' a macroeconomist could project. Sample surveys too are usually designed to tell about the average. In many developing countries, little is quantified about inequality at all.

Unfortunately, inequality is critical to knowing what to do about climate policy. The reason is that economic (and other) damages to poor people are worse than similar-sized damages to richer people. Richer, healthier people can better cope with the loss. They can more easily afford to sacrifice a little to prevent climate change too. Princeton University's Climate Futures Initiative – the same team of co-authors with which I investigated convergence between rich and poor countries – made a different modification to Nordhaus's model, to investigate inequality within countries around the world.

Nordhaus's IAM treats each country as one added-up whole. India is different from Japan, but everyone in India is the same and everyone in Japan is the same. This may be a reasonable initial assumption, but the Princeton team wanted to know how big a difference it would make to recognize just a little bit of inequality within countries. Like Shoibal Chakravarty's study, they split each population into five economic groups.

They tweaked the model to investigate two types of assumptions. First, they instructed the model to assume that the effects of climate change fell disproportionately on the poorer people within countries. In other words, they assumed that a warmer future would hurt poorer people more than richer people.

Then, they asked the model to assume that mitigation policy cost poorer people more than richer people. Here, they were investigating the implications of present-day environmental sacrifices falling harder on the poor than on the rich.

These new assumptions made all the difference. If the *harm* caused by climate change is going to fall mainly on the poorer people within each country, then decarbonisation is an urgent priority. In that case, climate change is worse than we thought: the model recommends aggressive mitigation policy. On the other hand, if the *costs* of reducing CO_2 emissions fall mainly on the poor, then the model recommends much less aggressive climate mitigation policy. Ignoring inequality within countries turns out to ignore a factor that could plausibly swing the ideal climate policy in either direction.

Yet again, this is a way in which development policy and environmental policy work together. The best climate policy would protect today's poor from paying the costs of reducing emissions and would protect the disadvantaged people in the future decades from suffering the worst of extreme temperatures. The problem is, nobody can quite be sure what path inequality is going to take. One reason is the limits of what economic science knows about inequality. A bigger reason is politics.

Governments could design climate mitigation policies in which the rich pay the costs, such as large taxes on airplane flights and luxury cars. An overall tax on carbon emissions could even make poor people *better off*, if the proceeds of the tax are invested in human development, or simply redistributed equally to everybody.

It is also easy to imagine mitigation policies that hurt poor people. Taxes on fossil fuels could, for example, make clean cooking fuel (such as LPG) more expensive. If so, more people will keep burning traditional fuels such as dung. More children will be harmed by the smoke. In India, we may not need to worry about this particular risk, because LPG is highly regulated – in practice, it is distributed by the state at least as much as by markets. As we saw in the last chapter, electricity is politically allocated too.

The implication is that the politics of who pays for climate mitigation could be as important as how much emission reduction happen. India has long worried, in international climate discussions, that reducing CO_2 pollution would hurt the Indian poor. But that does not have to happen: among other options is the possibility of a carbon tax with revenue recycled to the poor. French President Emmanuel Macron's 2018 petrol tax was countered by protests from the working class; the same environmental benefits would have been achieved while improving equality if the funds were visibly invested in social welfare or simply split equally among citizens. How much we should reduce emissions depends on who is paying for it. Who pays for emission reductions will be decided by the domestic politics of each country.

What if the world does not cooperate?

Nordhaus's models are designed to solve for a single, global pattern of optimal carbon taxes. There was a time when policymakers might have hoped that the world would come together for just such a collaborative, ideal solution. But, these days, international climate cooperation feels politically remote.

To clarify, just because the ideal climate policy would be cooperative does not imply that each country would do the same thing at the same time. Again, inequality matters. Richer countries can afford to reduce their carbon emissions without making their populations meaningfully worse off at all. In the poorest countries, emissions will remain useful in producing well-being and human development, probably for decades to come. But, an economic model that tries to maximize the world's stock of *money* cares most about the fact that rich countries already have useful, productive machinery. If you ask Nordhaus's model how to maximize the size of the economic pie, it will want to allow the richest economies to continue polluting.

A better question is to ask Nordhaus' model to maximize the world's *well-being*, now and in the future. These are not the same question, because global inequality is not disappearing any time soon. With the goal of maximizing well-being, the model computes that, in the best, collaborative policy, different countries will decarbonize at different times: the US and Europe almost immediately, India over the next several decades into the 21st century, and sub-Saharan Africa even a few decades after that. Such a plan offers the best balance of good lives for poorer people now and avoids suffering for everyone in the future.

Unfortunately, the world is far from the optimal plan. Since 2015, the Paris Agreement has recognized the bottom-up nature of climate policy, rooted in domestic politics. Many observers now worry that the Paris pledges are insufficiently ambitious, inadequately implemented, or both. Donald Trump is making matters worse. India could not stop climate change even by fully eliminating its emissions, and yet, is highly vulnerable to changing temperature. For India, which must formulate its best response to the climate injustice of the developed world, understanding what to do in a deeply sub-optimal world is critical.

Rich country emissions are appalling. Now what?

Lest there be any doubt, let me repeat: it is an ethical outrage for the rich countries not to decarbonize promptly and meaningfully fund the climate policies of the developing world. Moreover, even if India unilaterally eliminated all future emissions, it would hardly budge the full extent of climate change, unless other countries join in. Still, future Indians are even more vulnerable to climate change than is commonly understood.

The facts define a serious problem. It is a moral tragedy that India needs a strategic plan to protect the interests of future Indians from international emissions. In this, India is not alone: climate change is about moral tragedies.

If there is any clear implication, it may be that securing international climate cooperation should be among India's top foreign policy priorities. That would not be costless: promoting one priority means demoting others. Diplomats and security strategy experts might have to retool, turning their attention to learning something new. It might feel wrong: making nice with self-serving polluters, if that turns out to be the best strategy, could be an unpleasant way to protect the interests of future generations. It also might not succeed: for the time being, Donald Trump is among those on the other side of the table. Sometimes, the best options are bad instead of worse.

Of course, it is possible that making nice is not the only strategy to consider. A political scientist once suggested to me that India's best strategic response to climate change might be to stop complying with the international ozone treaty until the West gets serious about climate mitigation. As the conversation got going, we realized that it might be simpler just to pay Trump's son-in-law a few billion dollars.

Political scientists call this strategy 'issue linkage': if India wants the rich countries to change their climate policy, maybe it can apply pressure by *bundling* other policy issues where India has something to negotiate with. Some economists, for example, suggest that trade policy and tariffs could be used to punish countries that do not comply with international climate policies.

It would be a question for political creativity to imagine the best linkage to try. The point is only that this sort of international politics should be a top priority.

The options may be few. The consequences are uncertain. But the stakes are too high not to be taken seriously.

6

Co-benefits and Coal

In rural Raebareli, people as old as Gaurav have seen life get much better over the decades. 'We used to have to walk around in mud up to our ankles, but now we have these roads.' He is right about the roads. Although it was not the road he meant, I have felt the improvements, over the years, in the nearby highway from Lucknow to Allahabad. Gaurav pointed to a handpump that was not there some decades before. The National Thermal Power Company had built his family a cement latrine. And now, he concluded his list, we have some electricity.

We were chatting near a government coal plant. A genuine dark cloud hung over us. From where Nikhil and I talked with Gaurav, we could see three old smokestacks. A fourth one – newer and taller – was under construction. The plant, in the middle of Uttar Pradesh, is nowhere near coal mines; so large quantities of coal were constantly arriving by train. Indeed, half of the work that the Indian Railways does is transporting coal. Their revenue from moving coal is more than the price of all the tickets bought by passengers.

For Gaurav, all of that is the background. He explained that the smoke would turn a white shirt black on a clothesline, but this fact did not bother or interest him. We had been brought to his house by some villagers who figured that if we wanted to talk about the coal plant, we should ask our questions to someone they referred to as 'uncle' and his prominent family. Gaurav's son joined the conversation and had a more definite opinion about the coal plant: it would be better if it gave jobs to UP-wallahs like him, instead of people brought in from outside.

We asked if they would accept the smoke and pollution from another wing of the coal plant, if it meant that they would have electricity twenty-four hours a day. At first, the young man was against it. Leave things be: 'Nowhere in Uttar Pradesh is there twenty-four-hour electricity.' But Gaurav thought it would be a good idea. So, his son began enumerating costs and benefits, summing up with the English word 'fifty–fifty.'

Ambivalence about coal is understandable in India. For all of the fights over hydroelectric dams and promises of modern nuclear power, India has long fuelled its economic development by burning coal. Because Indian soil contains coal, the fuel has nationalist appeal: coal is available without depending on other countries. Coal is valuable to India's big-time politicians and small-time peddlers. It is worth fighting over, stealing, and entangling in corruption. But coal is a dirty fuel. It is responsible for much of India's particulate pollution and most of its carbon emissions. In 2010–11, Sarath Guttikunda and Puja Jawahar computed that air pollution from India's coal plants killed 80,000 to 1,15,000 people and caused 20 million cases of asthma.

The economics of coal is changing so fast that details could change between when I finish writing this book in January 2019 and when it is published a few months later. As technology advances, renewable energy is becoming an ever better economic deal. Wind and solar energy are ever-stronger competitors of coal, even on financial terms. So, coal is in a paradoxical limbo.

Its share of the world's total energy mix is declining. And yet, its share of world electricity generation is not.

In fact, global coal consumption went up in 2017 for the first time since 2013. India's increase in coal consumption was more than half of the whole world's increase. Coal produces more than three-fourths of India's electricity. As I write, India has much-needed plans to generate ever more electricity, including by burning coal.

The last chapter ground to a stop, trapped between two walls of a dilemma for climate policy. Blocking one side are the inescapable facts of India's climate vulnerability. Rising sea levels, heat and humidity, migration, and disrupted lives are all going to hit India hard – especially when compared with the countries that started the problem. The other side of the dilemma offers no way out: India cannot save itself merely by eliminating its own emissions. India's fate depends on decision makers in other countries. Many of these, unfortunately, have been unmoved by their own economies' responsibility. Giving up might seem tempting, but the threat is too severe. Those of us alive today have an obligation to future Indians to find or create the country's best response to this injustice.

The particles in Delhi's air block our view of the city – but they might show us an answer to the dilemma. We have seen how harmful particulate pollution is. Whether or not climate change were a threat, India would need to clear its air. Perhaps, with the very same policies, India can follow a path towards low-carbon economic development. If so, reducing carbon emissions would make present-day Indians better off (by reducing particulate air pollution), while positioning India as a leader internationally, ready to stimulate coordination to reduce future Indians' climate vulnerability.

If there is such an option, it would be a bit of good luck to build upon. But whether such an option exists depends on the details. Does any sort of polluting activity indeed cause particle pollution and carbon emissions at the same time? And is there anything that public policy and India's constrained governance could do about it?

How about starting with coal? The state burns it to generate electricity, so the state could do otherwise – if it can find or create other energy options to choose instead. So, we must turn to the details. Is there evidence that burning coal harms health now? What are its implications for climate change? For six chapters, air pollution and climate change have appeared to be two separate problems. In this chapter, the two halves of this book come together. Might the two problems have one solution? We already know that India cannot stop climate change merely by ending its own emissions – but there might be a more subtle opportunity in the details.

The costs of coal

The first step in answering these questions is to understand how harmful the pollution from burning coal might be. In Chapter 1, we learned that $PM_{2.5}$ threatens India's children. Burning coal causes $PM_{2.5}$ – most of it not directly, but in secondary chemical reactions between coal smoke and the air that it pollutes. Connecting the dots, we should expect an effect of burning coal on health in the important years at the start of life.

As always, finding and matching useful sources of data is the challenge. The best evidence that burning coal harms health is from scientists' understanding of each link in the causal chain. We know what coal plants emit; we know that it becomes small particles in the air; we know what inhaling tiny particles does to humans. Dozens and dozens of studies around the world have sorted out these details. Still, it would be nice for attracting political attention in India to have what economists call 'reduced form' evidence from Indian data. These are statistics that link variation in the root cause to variation in the final effect, even if each step is not visible.

Sangita – my collaborator at r.i.c.e. – realized that the same demographic survey data that we used together in Chapter 1 could also be used to track down the effect of coal plants. Recall the key advantage of that data: a representative sample of mothers throughout India reported each time they had ever given birth. The mothers' answers collectively tell us about hundreds of thousands of children. These children were born in different times, but in the same tens of thousands of villages and urban blocks.

Consider a district where a coal plant was built or expanded. Sangita's data could be used to compare children born *after* the coal plant with similar children born in the same district *before* the new coal plant. But districts without new coal plants are needed too. That is because, on average, health in India is improving. So, districts that do not gain any new coal plants can be used to account for unrelated patterns of change over time.

Accounting for changes in this way matters. Sangita found that children who live in districts that have a coal plant are taller, on average, than children who live in districts that do not have a coal plant. But coal plants are not allocated in a randomized experiment, like pills in a clinical trial. Quite the opposite; power plants are carefully placed by government decisions based on economic activity and engineering details. The industrial city of Kanpur has one; the rural people of Sitapur do not.

This is why studying *changes* was important to Sangita's strategy. She could account for the fact that some districts are enduringly better off than others by learning from the places where exposure to coal pollution changes. She used the rest of

India to account for changes in child health that were likely to happen even without a large new polluter. With Sagnik's computations of $PM_{2.5}$ from satellite measurements, Sangita double-checked that particle pollution increases where and when a new coal plant opens – so children should feel the effects.

Sangita found that when a new coal plant comes to a district, the children who are born afterwards are a little shorter, on average, than they otherwise would be. In Sangita's statistics, bigger coal plants with more capacity have bigger effects. Like most individual links in the population health chain, the effect on any one child is not enormous. After all, most children do not live right next to a large coal plant. But as always, the effects add up.

Coal plants are few, relative to the many other forces that cause the height of Indian children to vary. So, we can be more certain that there *is* an effect than we can be about the numbers of the *size* of the effect. For the children who are exposed to a new, average-sized coal plant, the cost to their height is in the same range as other big differences in child height that demographers have studied. It is about half as large as India's famous height shortfall relative to sub-Saharan Africa. The effect of an average new coal plant appearing in your district is about one-sixth as large as the difference between the height of the richest 20 per cent of Indian children and the poorest 20 per cent.

It makes sense that Sangita found effects of coal plants on public health in India. That is because effects are known to exist on *mortality* in other countries that adequately keep records of deaths. Remember the challenge of environmental health research in India: births and deaths are not registered. Decades ago, the US was economically closer to today's developing countries, but also was administratively advanced enough to maintain credible vital registration. So, researchers who are interested in the effects of coal plants could look to this period in the developing history of the US.

That is what Karen Clay and her economist co-authors did. They tracked US counties over time from 1938 to 1962, 'when emissions were virtually unregulated', according to the authors. In particular, they studied the consequences for infant mortality when a new coal-fired plant opened in a county. By 1962, Clay and co-authors found, burning coal to generate electricity 'was responsible for 3,500 infant deaths per year, over one death per thousand live births'.

In other words, burning coal harmed health. But it also had economic benefits, especially in places that did not initially have high rates of electrification. As a result, the economists' statistical strategy had to separate the benefits of electricity from the costs of burning coal. So, some of their analysis focused on cases when a coal plant was added to a county where people already had electricity. There, any statistical effect would isolate the consequences of burning coal, because electrification had already happened. In these cases, they found that a new coal plant in the county *lowered* housing values and rental prices.

One way to sharpen statistical conclusions is to study changes in the same people over time. To see the advantage of this approach, consider the alternative. The evidence from Chapter 1 about child height compared children born in places and times with more air pollution against children born in places and times with cleaner air. In other words, different children were compared, who were exposed to different levels of pollution. Our research team did everything it could to ensure that we were comparing apples to apples – that children only differed, on average, because of the pollution in the air. But we might have overlooked something. There might be some factor that we did not understand that coincidentally matches the pattern of exposure to pollution. If so, such a factor could mislead our conclusions.

Instead of comparing different children exposed to different levels of pollution, sometimes it is possible to compare changes over time in the experiences of the same people. Perhaps a group of people is exposed to low levels of pollution at one time in their lives and high levels at another. If somebody measured their health at both times, a researcher might be able to learn from the difference. Unfortunately, when data of any kind is scarce, such measurements of the same person twice over are especially hard to come by.

In Chapter 3, Aashish Gupta was my collaborator who realized that stoves in a village matter for the neighbours' health. Before he was studying stoves, Aashish was worrying about smoke from coal plants. Aashish and I wondered whether we could learn about the effects of coal pollution on health from the India Human Development Survey, known as the IHDS. The IHDS is one of the few surveys that asks the same people in India about their health at several points in their lives. The IHDS is built around a representative sample of 40,000 households throughout India. Surveyors asked these families about how life was going in 2005, and then again seven years later in 2012.

About one in ten of those households live in a district that gained or expanded a coal plant over those seven years. Aashish and I computed the average change in reported respiratory health among the households whose districts gained a coal plant. We also found the average change in health among households living in a place that reached 2012 with as many coal plants nearby as in 2005. Because the IHDS asks pages of questions – about economic wealth, jobs, education, and more – Aashish and I could verify that we were not being misled by coincidental changes in any of these other parts of the 40,000 families' lives.

On average, Indians were healthier in 2012 than in 2005: they were less likely to report recently being troubled by a cold or cough. But people living in districts that gained a coal plant did not see such an improvement. People whose exposure to coal smoke increased were a little more likely in 2012 than they were in 2005 to tell a surveyor that they had respiratory health problems. Families living in the rest of India, in contrast, became a little less likely to report a cough. The same families were interviewed in 2005 and in 2012. So, Aashish and I could be confident that this pattern was not, for example, because of changes in who decides to live near a coal plant or in an industrialized area.

The IHDS did not only ask about coughs. We saw an effect of coal plants on reported coughs, but not on reported diarrhoea or reported fever. So, the effect was only on the outcome we would most expect: respiratory health. Similarly, Aashish and I only found an effect of *coal* plants in particular. There was no effect of new power plants of other types, such as hydroelectric plants or wind power, which do not cause air pollution. The fact that the pattern is specific to coal plants and respiratory health is persuasive: living near so many coal plants is bad for Indians' health.

Co-benefits: When two problems have one solution

Burning coal is well-known to be a major source of greenhouse gas emissions, causing climate change. Coal is responsible for the majority of India's carbon emissions. Burning coal already harms thousands of people's health today. India burns a lot of coal. Climate scientists have a word for the opportunity presented by the combination of these three facts: co-benefits.

From the point of view of a climate scientist, reducing coal consumption would have the *benefit* of scaling back the harm that climate change does. Reducing coal would have the *co-benefit* of improving health today. Burning coal causes two types of harmful externality: one for climate-vulnerable future Indians, and another for the health and growth of India's children today. A climate policy is said to have 'co-benefits' for human development if it improves something else while reducing carbon emissions. Because burning coal causes both short-term and long-term externalities, reducing coal consumption promises both benefits (eventually) and co-benefits (for health now).

In the last chapter, we were left with what appeared to be an unsolvable puzzle. India has every reason to reduce its exposure to harm from climate change. But, India has almost no reason to reduce only its own CO_2 emissions, because doing so would have such a small effect on temperature changes. Health co-benefits give India a different type of reason to reduce CO_2 emissions, at least to the point that is justified by protecting the health of Indians today. And perhaps, if India is strategic about it, doing so would be just the contribution to climate cooperation that India would need to make in order to position itself as a collaborator in its calls for richer countries to do their part too. Even that might not work, especially as long as the party of Donald Trump controls the United States. But the key fact is that it would not cost anything to try, on net, because of the large and present costs of continuing to burn coal. Reducing emissions in this way, by this amount, would improve India's health, its economy, and maybe its position in international politics.

It makes sense to focus on coal, because coal is so uniquely polluting. But reducing coal consumption is not the only environmental policy that might have co-benefits. Moreover, co-benefits have already been part of India's written climate aspirations for years. For example, the Government of India's 2008 National Action Plan on Climate Change called for tactics that 'promote our development objectives while also yielding co-benefits for addressing climate change effectively'. And yet, such a call is easy to proclaim without making any changes. 'Co-benefits' cannot be just a slogan; it is certainly not an excuse for development business as usual. Instead, it is an invitation to sort out the details. Exactly how much, and what type, of emission reductions would turn out to be in India's own collective self-interest?

So, co-benefits may be important to finding India's best response to climate injustice. Now we need to know about the numbers. How do the costs of particles in the air now and the costs of climate change in the future stack up – when added together – against the costs of switching to cleaner sources of power?

As usual, there is another wrinkle. It is not quite so simple as noticing that burning coal causes both carbon emissions and disease. The complication is that particles in the air can cool the earth. Think of north India in the winter: picture how dim and grey the days are for us humans on the ground. Light – with its warming energy from the sun – bounces off the particles in the air. $PM_{2.5}$ particles are small, but they are much larger than molecules of CO_2, which stay up in the air much longer. In a scientific irony, one of the effects of particle pollution is to make the earth, on net, a little cooler.

Understanding all implications of particle pollution would require balancing effects on the economy, on health, and on the climate – for warmer and for cooler. This task fell to Noah Scovronick, Mark Budolfson, and our collaborators. Noah, Mark, and I are members of the Climate Futures Initiative: the team of co-authors from Chapter 5, led from Princeton University. Noah is a public health scientist, trained in the statistics of epidemiology. Just before I met him, he was living in South Africa, studying environmental health. Before that, he had investigated whether poor people's houses in the slums around Cape Town are adequate to protect them from the weather. Mark studies environmental policy; his expertise is in the paradoxes of responsibility for problems that many people cause together. The rest of our international team includes an engineer, computer modellers, several economists, and Fabian Wagner, an atmospheric scientist who had won a prestigious mathematics prize when he was studying at Cambridge.

Noah and the Climate Futures Initiative team went back to the climate-economy model of Bill Nordhaus, the 2018 Nobel laureate. Nordhaus's model offered the rails and the engine to compute a comparison of all the costs, benefits and co-benefits of pollution. Noah's task was to find a way to attach health externalities caused by air pollution: more cars in Nordhaus's train.

The team got to work. Each step used different expertise. One car in the train was the effect of climate mitigation on particulate air pollution. Our computer model needed to know by how much particle concentrations would be reduced, as a by-product of policies to reduce carbon emissions. The next car translated particle concentrations to health consequences. This step used the type of statistical evidence we saw in Chapter 1: estimates of the impact of exposure to ambient particles on mortality. Finally, our last new train car translated health damages into an equivalent economic loss. The economic loss could be balanced against the economic costs and benefits of climate mitigation policy. Globally, air pollution tends to be more severe in poorer countries than in richer countries. So, the model incorporated an assumption that is standard to economists: that the same loss is more important to the evaluation of a policy if the loss is suffered by a poorer person, rather than a richer person.

Before these cars could be linked to Nordhaus's train, Noah and the team had to tune up an imbalance in the engine.

Recognizing only the health costs of particulate pollution would be unfairly tipping the balance in favour of environmental regulation. To make it fair, we needed to also incorporate the cooling effect of particles in the air. Because Nordhaus's original model was about greenhouse gas – not ambient particles – it ignored this *benefit* of air pollution. The modelling team set up a switch in the tracks. We could follow Nordhaus's original model, or add only the cooling effects of air particles (ignoring health co-benefits). Or, we could use the most complete version of the model, incorporating both cooling effects and health consequences.

Unsurprisingly, setting the switch to only recognize the cooling effects of particulate pollution results in the model recommending a much less ambitious policy response to climate change. This makes sense: if pollution has an unrecognized benefit, then recognizing the benefit would amount to a reason to allow more pollution. So far, so good, this test of the model showed.

Resetting the switch to incorporate health co-benefits produces dramatic results. The recommended climate policy becomes much more aggressive. Optimal emissions are lower than the results we find without considering health. The target date for decarbonisation moves decades sooner. Two-hundred-and sixty-eight gigatons less carbon is emitted to the atmosphere, over the coming decades, under the policy recommendation that properly recognizes health co-benefits, relative to a benchmark policy recommendation that does not. With emissions so much lower, the peak global temperature change is almost half a degree lower.

The bottom line of all of this macroeconomic modelling is that health co-benefits make a decisive difference to what the best climate policy should be. This conclusion is especially true for India. The Princeton models of the climate and the economy come in a range of variants and flavours. They repeatedly show that India has much to gain from climate policy that takes co-benefits seriously (often the most to gain of any region, in fact).

Sagnik and Sourangsu – my collaborators from Chapter 1 – teamed up with Kirk Smith, the air pollution expert who studied stoves in Chapter 4, to calculate how important health co-benefits could be for India in particular. They projected exposure to $PM_{2.5}$ in India under two scenarios for global climate policy. One is a relatively optimistic scenario, under which climate policy becomes more aggressive and succeeds in limiting the worst consequences. The other is a pessimistic scenario, under which the world continues merely to talk about reducing carbon emissions, but allows temperatures to rise.

What is important about Sagnik, Sourangsu, and Kirk's estimates is that (like Noah's economic model) they focus on a choice between two *climate* policy paths, not two particulate policies. And yet, they find a large difference in future Indians' exposure to airborne particles. Under the more ambitious climate policy scenario, particulate pollution becomes lower around 2040 than it is today. Under the less ambitious scenario, particulate pollution remains above even present-day highs until near the beginning of the next century. In that case, Delhi, Haryana and Uttar Pradesh would suffer higher pollution levels until the year 2100 than today's levels. As a result, India's premature mortality because of particulate pollution is 30 per cent higher in the scenario in which climate change is not tackled. Co-benefits matter.

Could two solutions do even better? Only in theory

For the last time, we must return to the old-fashioned debate about whether economics is opposed to environmental policy. It is not. Pollution is the textbook example of an externality;

an externality generates economic inefficiency; every economics textbook agrees that policy must correct the inefficiency caused by the externality. If policymakers instead let the free market pollute as much as it wants to, the economy does worse than it could. Nordhaus won an economics Nobel for constructing a system to compute the details; Noah and company added an important gear to that system.

'But wait!' – an economic theorist interjects – 'particulate pollution and climate change are two different problems. The optimal policy solution must therefore use two different policy instruments.' In theory, the complaint is right. Setting greenhouse gas policy in a way that recognizes present-day health consequences is better than ignoring present-day health consequences. However, better yet would be a more complicated package of policies: choosing the optimal scheme to regulate particulate pollution and the optimal scheme to control CO_2 emissions.

This idea won a Nobel prize too. In 1969, Jan Tinbergen shared the first economics Nobel prize, in part for a theoretical insight that has remained at the heart of public economics. To reach the best possible outcome, each distortion or inefficiency – that is to say, each factor that moves an economy away from the ideal situation in which decision makers bear the costs of their own pollution – requires its own policy tool, such as a tax on pollution. So, the very best economic outcome would only happen with a mix of two policies – that is, only if the government combined the best regulation of CO_2 with the best regulation of particulate pollution.

Noah, Mark and the Princeton programmers were aware of this fact from economic theory. But, they instead asked Nordhaus's model a *combined* question: 'Imagine that you had to choose *one* emissions control policy, knowing that it would influence both future climate change and how many particles pollute today's air. All things considered, what one emissions control policy would you choose?' Asking this question was not a mistake because, in the world beyond economists' theories and computer models, policymaking often has to kill two birds with one stone. A clear answer emerged to this question: the one emissions control policy should limit pollution and carbon emissions.

Having established this, the Princeton team decided to be thorough. They ran their computer program again, allowing it to optimize both climate policy and particulate pollution policy. Economic theory tells us that, in this case, the total efficiency and welfare of the economy would have been higher. The computer still found that it made sense to reduce carbon emissions, because it still had the benefit of making people healthier – although not by quite as much.

The implication is that, even allowing two levers of policymaking – one for climate change and one for air pollution – the co-benefits of reducing air pollution add up to a good reason for India to reduce carbon emissions. But if there is only one lever – if both problems have to be solved with the same plan – then the argument for reducing emissions is especially strong. And in the real world of limited state capacity, this is the case that matters.

If it does not work in practice, it does not work

History has shown that it is possible to reduce particulate pollution in the air while increasing carbon emissions. Europe did it. The 'great London smog' of 1952 was no more a matter of mere precipitation than is the 'fog' that slows trains passing through Uttar Pradesh. It was pollution and smoke. When the UK Parliament issued a ban on burning coal in London in

1956, the air cleared. But over the 20th century, greenhouse gas emissions in the UK continued.

China achieved the same dubious honour more recently. One reason why India's cities now appear at the top of the 'most polluted' list is that China cleaned up its air. Concerted government effort was enough to achieve 'blue skies over Beijing', as the title of a recent book by Matthew E. Kahn and Siqi Zheng summarizes.

India is not China, and neither is it the 20th century UK. India must address its air pollution challenges with the governance resources available to a much weaker state. A solution that will not be implemented or will not be enforced will not make anyone breathe easier.

Ours is not the theoretically optimal world. It is nice to know what the ideal policy – rich in all of its details and complexity – could achieve. But what we really need to know is what to do. Which policies that might actually be implemented should those of us who care about India's children and future generations advocate for? Not a theoretical optimum that exists only on an economist's chalkboard. The best plan must be workable. That means planning around the fact that India is not going to pursue the optimal set of complex regulations, one for each pollutant. Finding the best plan means looking for a good policy that is simple enough to happen.

It may even be technically feasible, in theory, to regulate a system of monitoring and filters. But doing so is expensive – especially when renewable energy is only becoming ever cheaper. More importantly, to *enforce* requirements that polluting plants clean their air would depend on a commitment to and capacity for regulation on which India should not bet lives. Optimal regulations, expressed in detailed quantitative limits of each chemical, work great on the blackboard – but nowhere else in India.

Unfortunately, India has a history of announcing regulations on pollution from coal plants – and then ignoring them. For example, in 2015 the Government of India announced regulations on SO_2 emissions from coal plants. Complying with these rules, while continuing to operate an old coal plant, would be expensive. Anish Sugathan and co-authors estimate the hypothetical cost of total compliance at Rs 75 billion per year, nation-wide. Unfortunately, as these authors summarize: 'Despite the stringent timelines and limits set by the newer standards, there has been slow progress in the adoption of the sulphur control norms – an estimated 90 per cent coal power plants continue to violate the emission norms by the first compliance deadline of December 7, 2017.'

The response of the Central Electricity Authority to these violations was to extend the deadline for compliance until 2024. Among missed opportunities to control pollution, this one may not even be the worst: at least ignoring the deadline became the official government policy. Often in environmental governance – as we will see in the next chapter – improperly allowing rules to be ignored and pollution to continue is a decision that individual inspectors make on the spot. Nobody ever officially admits it. A theoretical response to climate change or air pollution that ignores these governance constraints may sound as nice as 'clean coal', but actually be little better than no response at all.

A simple option: The end of coal

Environmental policy is full of buts and yets and caveats. Consequences are complicated. Most proposals help some people, hurt others, and add up to big changes through many tiny effects. Surrounded by all these details, we have come to a simple conclusion – good for Indians today, good for Indians of the future, a sensible domestic policy, and reasonable in international dialogue.

The Indian state should stop burning coal.

This is a policy book built on social science. It is not an engineering manual. I will not pretend to offer technical details about which coal boiler should be turned off in which year, or exactly how quickly coal should be phased out. What everybody needs to know is the big picture conclusion: planning and working for an accelerated end of coal should be a top policy priority.

That conclusion may not mean turning off all coal plants tomorrow, but it certainly means formulating wise plans for them to be off soon. (And it might mean turning off some of them tomorrow: Dan Tong and co-authors investigated 'super-polluting' coal plants around the world in a 2018 study. They found that the worst 7 per cent of India's coal plants offer only 1.8 per cent of the country's electricity generating capacity, but are responsible for 13 per cent of $PM_{2.5}$ pollution from coal.)

It also means not building new coal plants or investing in their physical capital. India plans to expand its coal-fired capacity in the coming years by tens of gigawatts. Such an increase would be a large net increase over what it plans to retire – and would be despite the fact that plants today are running well below capacity because the grid cannot deliver the electricity.

New coal plants make little economic sense: investing in a durable power plant only is worth the upfront costs if it will operate for many years. Trends point towards a probability that renewables may soon be less expensive than burning coal, even in a coal plant that already exists. So, buying a new coal plant could mean sinking money into an asset with a short lifespan.

Finally, as bad as it is to burn coal, this chapter has said nothing about the social costs of *mining* coal, which are considerable as well. Coal mining in India is a classic 'resource curse': it disrupts politics and institution building by offering unearned wealth to fight over. Because so much of India's coal is found in eastern states where Adivasis live, coal mining displaces some of India's poorest, least powerful citizens.

To stop burning coal would have three benefits for India. First, the health benefits would be undeniable and are immediate, for today's population. Burning coal makes Indians unhealthy today and harms the development of the next generation. In other words, shifting investments to renewables may involve some economic costs, especially in the short term, but these costs can be more than outweighed by the health consequences of air pollution. Coal is not the only problem – remember the complexity of 'source apportionment' studies, and the harms caused by the smoke of traditional cooking stoves. But it is an obvious big step.

Second, phasing out coal is a simple plan that recognizes the reality of governance constraints. The Indian state does not have the capacity to implement the theoretically optimal set of regulations. More broadly, much that happens in India is outside of the control of the state. But much of the coal that is burnt in India is burnt by the government. Even coal plants that the government does not own, it has helped finance. Coal is the rare policy lever that the Indian state undeniably can pull.

Of course, some coal plants are not owned by the government, but instead by powerful corporations and business families. In some cases, the coal plant is merely one part of a vertically integrated organization that imports the coal, burns it, and uses it to fuel production. With coal power so linked with political power and economic power, it is no surprise that coal has been implicated in some of India's biggest corruption scandals. Unequal concentration of wealth has long been argued to have anti-democratic political externalities for everyone; in India, coal is part of that story. There may be little that the Indian state can be expected to do about these cases in the short run. But if so, the irresponsibility of private actors would be no excuse for the government to participate in generating coal pollution.

Another argument one sometimes hears for continuing to invest money in coal plants is that banks (including government banks) have *already* invested in coal plants. Such logic holds that hurting coal plants would also hurt the banks that invested in them. But this is not a good enough argument for producing pollutants that stunt children today and will kill others tomorrow. The problem with this argument is that it confuses private *financial* interests with public *economic* efficiency. It may be true that some people would lose money from a shift from coal – but even if so, other people would benefit by more. Because of health and other externalities, burning coal is not economically efficient for India overall.

More broadly, new technologies always cause winners and losers. As I tell my introductory economics students, you can tell that an economy is not efficient if nobody ever goes out of business. If the same powerful firms, families, or banks are always protected, then the 'free entry and exit' condition for economic efficiency is not met. In a free market, investors lose money for bad decisions. In this case, it may be defensible for the government to spend some of the efficiency gains from shifting out of coal on compensating banks and others who have invested in coal plants – but whether or not to do so is a political question, not an economic one.

Third and finally, India may be able to translate the end of coal into international policy leverage. The high-emissions rich countries are the bad guys of climate policies. But India is caricatured as a grumpy outsider for highlighting the facts of this injustice. Paying attention to health co-benefits would only ask Indians to do what is in their own self-interest. Yet, it could be enough to put India well within the global green team.

Nordhaus and other economists have shown that an in-group of environmentally responsible countries could use trade policy to fight climate change together. By agreeing to assign tariffs and other penalties, a 'climate club' of countries could collectively reward countries that cooperate with emissions reductions, while punishing countries that do not. No climate club exists yet – but India could help create one. A climate club would be another example of 'issue linkage': linking international climate politics to other cases where climate-vulnerable countries have more leverage.

Across a wide range of Nordhaus's computations, India emerges as a big winner from the existence of such an international club. That conclusion is no surprise in light of India's vulnerability to climate change. Merely doing as much as health co-benefits require – merely pursuing an economically efficient outcome – could position India as a leader of the club.

Renewables and reality

Even if burning coal is a terrible idea, India can only phase it out if there is an alternative to phase in. Nuclear power is, in principle, an option. But nuclear power offers only a few percentage points of India's electricity generation. Whether or not this is regrettable, it appears unlikely to change soon, relative to medium-term emissions goals. Sometimes I regret the practical and political implausibility of cheap, emissions-free nuclear power for India. But then I remember that the coal plant near Gaurav's house in Raebareli exploded last year, killing thirty-two people. And then I feel grateful that it was not a nuclear plant.

Switching out of coal will importantly mean switching into wind and solar. Just next to the Raebareli coal plant is a solar power plant. The solar plant is, in principle, capable of generating 10 MW. That capacity is 1 per cent of the 1000 MW capacity of the immediately neighbouring coal plant (which had another few hundred megawatts under construction when I talked with Gaurav).

I visited the solar plant on Independence Day. The ground around the solar panels was flooded with August rain. A shoe-destroying walk through the mud and water brought me to the control room in a small building. There, a cheerful young engineer from Bengaluru watched a bank of computer screens. A TV monitor reviewed a list of fifteen highlights of the Prime Minister's holiday speech that morning.

The control room was set up in a museum-like display. The apparent goal was to impress visitors with modern renewable energy and with colourful displays of General Electric–branded software. The young engineer was excited to show me the screens. He clearly wanted the message to be good.

It was not good. That cloudy day, most of the dots were red, not green. The screens reported that the solar plant was generating 60 kW. The engineer assured me that one day it had gotten up to 7500 kW. A megawatt is 1000 kilowatts. So, at 0.06 MW, the solar plant was producing less than 1 per cent of the 10 MW that the signboard at the entrance promised, which would have been 1 per cent of the coal plant.

It is not surprising that a solar plant does not generate much electricity if it is built beneath the smoke of a coal plant with 100 times the capacity. Ordinarily, one places solar plants in the path of direct sunlight. This one was placed in the path of visitors.

∽

If public investment were shifted out of coal, it could move to renewables. Solar panels now cost less than 1 per cent of what they did forty years ago. In the US, the cost of wind energy has fallen by about two-thirds since Barack Obama became president.

Although renewables are becoming a better option each year, almost everyone agrees that renewables are not yet fully ready to replace coal. Like coal plants, they operate below capacity. Solar and wind energy generation both have the problem of 'intermittency': they do not generate a constant flow of uniform power. But as E. Somanathan observes, some electricity demand, such as for irrigation, does not need to happen at any particular time. For these uses, intermittency is not a problem.

Part of investing in making renewables usable will be continuing to invest in India's electrical distribution grid. Another part will be the continued development of electricity storage technology. All of these problems are receiving attention and investment from researchers and companies around the world – including in India. The next breakthrough in electricity storage might come from a PhD dissertation at IIT. The energy sector should be watching for those breakthroughs, and stand ready to do the hard work of filling the gaps between a research discovery and a useable technology. (If *you* are an IIT PhD student, work towards the next breakthrough!)

Perhaps the 0.06 MW solar plant in Raebareli was merely having an off day when I visited. Even still, it warns of another challenge against hopes for renewables. The lesson is that it is easy to *pretend* to be moving to renewables. It is easy to pretend to be reducing pollution, shifting out of coal, investing in solar energy. It is easy to build a science museum display in a control room, or to arrange for a photo op of a politician with a windmill or a solar panel. But many large renewable generators are needed.

If plans to build new coal plants continue apace, if renewables remain a tiny part of the plant, then the pivot to renewables would be just for show. That might not be altogether bad. Over-optimistic talk about renewable energy could be an important part of building and participating in an international coalition for climate mitigation. Think of the 'climate clubs' that use trade policy to reward cooperating countries and punish defectors: optimistic talk could help, because nobody is going to join the club if they do not believe that there will be other cooperators. But optimistic talk only works if it translates into somebody changing something. In the meantime, the pollutants are real.

Part III
Policy or Pretence

7

Expert Performance

Kanpur does not wake up early. On a moist weekend morning in July 2018, overnight rains had left ponds of water, stagnant in the streets and paths. Not until around 8.30 a.m. would a woman in flip flops and a red sari – stained brown up to her knees – begin her work with the trash outside the district hospital. She pulled and pushed the trash into piles, using a garden hoe. Three dogs waited to see what she found. Few other people were out so early in downtown Kanpur, almost none of them women. Within the gates of the maternity hospital, the morning was a little livelier: milk was for sale from a Parag stall. There, a young man attended to a similar task, scooping trash into a wheelbarrow with a shovel. Much of that trash was used plastic bags, thrown into the parking lot.

Some Kanpuris woke up early that day. An hour and a half before anyone was scooping trash from the courtyard of the district hospital, a celebratory footrace would be held at the cricket stadium, according to a local newspaper. The race was to commemorate Uttar Pradesh's most recent ban of plastic bags. 'For the third time in the past three years,' the *Indian Express* also reported, 'the Uttar Pradesh government has banned polythene and plastic from Sunday' – specifically, disposable bags thinner than 50 microns. No citizens voted for such a bag ban: it happened because the Uttar Pradeshi legal and regulatory system thought it would be a good idea. 'Though it had taken the step earlier as well' – twice, the article details – 'the government failed to formulate any rule, leading to its failure.'

The race would be an out-and-back along VIP Road. The course ran from the cricket stadium to the turn at an intersection featuring a large, gold-coloured statue of B.R. Ambedkar, then back to the stadium: seven kilometres. VIP Road boasts a few fancy car dealerships and other high-status shops – as well as plenty of plastic bags heaped in sodden puddles. That morning, like every morning, men here and there pushed wheelbarrows, like the one at the district hospital, full of plastic bags of trash.

A week after the ban, Dinesh Raj Bandela wrote in *Down to Earth* magazine that a second-time offender caught using a plastic bag in Uttar Pradesh could be imprisoned for six months. Even on the first offence, possession of a plastic bag could be punishable with a month in prison. But Bandela, too, had worries about implementation. 'So far, several states have failed to implement plastic bans due to more than one reason: lack of cost-effective alternatives and a proper system to ensure segregation and disposal of plastic waste.' Bandela does not mention whether those states held footraces.

That morning, I missed the race. I started the day at the district hospital and did not read the newspaper in time. By the time I reached the cricket stadium at 11 a.m., there was little evidence that anything had happened. Disposable pink plastic bags littered the parking lot between the gate and the stadium entrance. A guard showed me around the stadium, pointing out where the players sat and where the media sat. Once, the stadium had hosted an international match! I asked about a plastic board in the corner, advertising the morning bag-ban event. He shrugged that it was over. I asked if anyone came. Sure, he said 300, 400 – the number kept growing – or 500 children.

Because I was not there, I do not know how many children or other people actually completed the seven-kilometre course described in the newspaper. This would be a long distance for untrained adult participants, even in clean air. A few times in a good week, I run that far in more than half an hour. But if Kanpur's one air quality monitor (three kilometres away from the course) reflects conditions on VIP Road, then $PM_{2.5}$ was 85. At such a high particle concentration, children should consider reducing prolonged or heavy exertion, according to the US Environmental Protection Agency. At the San Joaquin Valley's public schools in California, this level of $PM_{2.5}$ would trigger the condition: 'No outdoor activity. All activities should be moved indoors.' Because it was monsoon season, $PM_{2.5}$ was relatively low, as it goes in Kanpur.

As I walked out of the empty stadium grounds, another guard sat by the gate in a plastic chair. Squatting beneath him, a vendor carefully used a hanging balance to measure out a quantity of a toasted rice snack. He sold the snack to the stadium guard in a disposable plastic bag.

The inconvenience caused

The harm caused by air pollution is a fact. This chapter asks why policy responses to environmental challenges are often fiction and sometimes fantasy. Many of India's policy responses to pollution are constructed by administrators or courts, not by elected politicians. Such rules often involve quantitative or scientific details: 50 microns. How should we understand a ban that is not a ban? Is it a public aspiration? Or is it merely public indifference? If it is an act, who is it for? Is there an audience who knows enough to know what a micron is, but knows so little as to believe that such a ban would happen?

In January 2016, Delhi's drivers joined the act. For fifteen days, only cars with licence plates ending in odd numbers could drive on odd numbered days. Only cars ending in even numbers could drive on even days. Maybe it is just my friends, but any conversation I had about the ban included the joke that it is easy to buy two licence plates. A few days into the ban, the joke had intensified: ads for arranged marriages would now start including car numbers.

Behind the sarcasm is the serious fact that any major regulation creates a large incentive to avoid it. Everybody assumed it would be evaded. But marriage ads never moved from joking to reality, because the odd–even scheme was never a major regulation. Within the fifteen days, the rule only applied form 8 am to 8 pm – and not on Sunday. Among the exemptions were women, two-wheelers, school buses, and all manners of public or administrative vehicles. The scheme annoyed some people and dominated the news – but did it do anything about air pollution?

Sourangsu, Sagnik and Sachi had the satellite pictures to find out. Along with three other co-authors, they analysed data on pollution from satellite measurements. The scientific team compared pollution during the odd–even scheme with pollution in the prior thirteen years. They soften their conclusions in scientific language: 'not a significant result', 'not detected', 'within the uncertainty range'. In a scientific journal, such polite verbiage is damning. Nothing happened.

An economist named Michael Greenstone and his co-authors also studied the results of the odd–even scheme. They used a different strategy. They consulted ten air quality monitors at various points in Delhi, some located where odd–even might help and some not. Their conclusions depend on exactly how the statistics are computed. Combining the January scheme with a repeat in April does not find any effect. But there is some evidence of a small effect – a 13 per cent decrease in pollution – if one concentrates only on January, only on daytime hours, at these monitoring stations. However, during that same January in Delhi, Sangita measured that air pollution was worst overnight or in the very early morning – not during the hours when odd and even were supposed to apply.

So, for all the attention it received, the odd–even scheme accomplished little or nothing for cleaner air. In their discussion of their findings, Sourangsu and co-authors seem (politely) exasperated that anybody might have thought this would achieve anything, let alone constitute an 'emergency measure'. The scheme was tiny relative to the problem: 'the bulk of pollution that lingers outside the [Delhi city] limits will not be contained outside the boundaries of the city if the traffic interventions are applied only within' Delhi.

One possibility is that the odd–even scheme was a mistake. Another possibility is that it achieved its goals: it generated two weeks of news assertions that the government was doing something. If so, the inconvenience caused was the point.

Who is fooling whom?

The odd–even driving scheme was never going to solve air pollution. The solar plant in the last chapter was built under the smoke of a coal plant with over 100 times its peak capacity. It was never a serious transition to renewable energy. Without close inspection, however, any of these programmes and policies might have seemed to be something that they never were. In each case, the state pretended to do something about a difficult problem: pollution, carbon emissions, or plastic bags.

India's voters do not live in the only country where the state sometimes pretends to responsibly manage environmental health. For example, Paulina Oliva, an economics professor, investigated emission testing of cars in Mexico. All but six of the eighty emissions testers that she audited in Mexico City accepted a bribe to report that a car passed emissions tests when it did not.

China is an important example, because its pollution levels have recently improved. Dalia Ghanem and Junjie Zhang are two economists who studied the data on air pollution that local governments in China report to the central government. Ghanem and Zhang recognized that local officials have career incentives to report clear days. 'Local officials are expected to comply with the environmental standards because their prospects for career advancement are linked to their ability to meet the targets set by the higher-level offices. In addition, local officials compete with each other on observable performance measures, including economic output and social stability, creating a promotion tournament.' Ghanem and Zhang saw that this sort of arrangement creates an economic motivation to report good news – whether true particle counts justify it or not.

Each day's level of particle pollution depends on many random factors, such as the wind. So, pollution counts across days have a smooth statistical distribution. But a plot of the reports that Chinese cities make about their pollution is not smooth. The pattern breaks in a large jump at exactly the threshold that mattered for local officials' rewards. No natural variation could create such a pattern: the officials were cheating. However, in part because the cheating was documented, the rules changed. Later research by Thomas Stoerk, an environmental economist, argues that the jump has disappeared. Even more importantly, China's example shows that corruption can coexist with progress. Despite this particular pattern of dishonesty, there is wide agreement that public policy has led to large reductions in particle pollution in China.

Nor is air pollution the only target of public pretence. Governments lie all the time. When writer Isaac Asimov reviewed George Orwell's *1984* from the viewpoint of 1980, it felt silly to him that the novel had devoted so much attention to the detailed manipulation of facts and statistics. Who cares about that stuff? 'As any politician knows, no evidence of any kind is ever required,' Asimov understood. 'It is only necessary to make a statement – any statement – forcefully enough to have an audience believe it. No one will check the lie against the facts, and, if they do, they will disbelieve the facts. Do you think the German people in 1939 pretended that the Poles had attacked them and started World War II? No! Since they were told that was so, they believed it as seriously as you and I believe that they attacked the Poles.'

This chapter asks why anyone would bother to build last chapter's miniature solar plant, separated from the sun by a coal plant's smoke. Why construct a display that claims that the plant produces 10 megawatts? Who is the audience for whom that act is performed? More importantly, what are the consequences? Does appearing to protect the environment generate the optimism and expectations that are needed to sustain cooperation? If so, a little deception would in fact be an act of wise leadership. But there is another possibility: fake policymaking could crowd out demand for the genuine article. If so, Indians would continue to suffer from pollution for decades after the Chinese state (and others) managed to clear the air.

Development in our times is paradoxical. On one side of the paradox is the pretence of management. Governments and development agencies claim to be micromanaging poverty, health, education, and industrialization for the detailed greater good. Often, these claims are a response to expectations that others place on the state: development agencies, news media, and professors' books all proceed under the assumption that poor states can, should, and will manage the solutions to very hard problems. So, each project in a long list comes with a number-laden study of its benefits. In general, these go unread and unbelieved. In the meantime, infant deaths and child stunting are real.

The other side of the paradox is that such anarchy does not spell disaster, even though most important trends are outside of bureaucratic control. Just the opposite: lives are improving. My own research, for example, studies the health of children. We can see the puzzle here. A much larger fraction of Indian children is born in hospitals or clinics than were fifteen years ago. This change may appear to be the explanation for a very welcome trend: infant mortality in Uttar Pradesh and Bihar is lower than ever before. But children born in health facilities in these states are no more likely to survive the start of life than are comparable children born at home. Not in recent data, not in older data. The expanding reach of the healthcare system does not appear to be responsible for India's ongoing, rapid decline in early-life mortality.

As long as well-being continues to race ahead, it might be harmless that policy is so much pretence: a merely regrettable missed opportunity. Official business as usual can afford to be indifferent to the truth if matters are anyway improving. The trouble is that air pollution and climate change are both getting worse. The market will not stop it, because pollution is always a market failure. In India, its endurance has hardened it into a government failure too. Pretending to address the problem could plausibly help or could plausibly hurt. This matters because the atmosphere will not heal on its own.

Does change need lies?

The history of deception from high political places is long. For many Americans, faith in government assertions never recovered from the 1971 release of the Pentagon Papers. If the badness of a lie depends on the size of the issue, then the US government's lies about the Vietnam War were terrible. Totalling over more than a decade, between 1–3 million people died in the Vietnam War, according to various estimates that count civilian and military deaths on all sides. These numbers are large, but they are not much greater, if at all and in rough magnitude, than India's *annual* count of deaths from air pollution.

The Pentagon Papers were piles of Defence Department documents, stolen and given to the press by Daniel Ellsberg. (I first learned about Ellsberg, in my training in mathematical economics, as an accomplished choice theorist). The Pentagon Papers revealed that the government's best and brightest had long understood that the Vietnam War was unwinnable. Rather than stop the killing, they lied to the voters and juked the stats.

Hannah Arendt was a philosopher of government who was born in Germany but moved to New York in 1941. She is most famous for what she wrote in the 1950s and 1960s on totalitarianism and Nazi Germany. Writing in 1971, later in her life, she was not as surprised by the Pentagon Papers as others were. 'Secrecy… and deception, the deliberate falsehood and outright lie used as legitimate means to achieve political ends, have been with us since the beginning of recorded history. Truthfulness has never been counted among the political virtues, and lies have always been regarded as justifiable tools in political dealings.'

Arendt scathes the 'problem-solvers' whose 'undoubted intelligence', 'eager to find formulas' produced the Pentagon papers. But her reflections stand out, in part, for a possibility that she raises along the way: that there sometimes is a decent purpose to lying in politics. The purpose of politics is to change the world. To change the world, we have to imagine it differently. For everyone to imagine it differently, the politician must *describe* it differently. If you are a good politician, you can get people to go along with you. Assume the change you want to see in the world – and talk about it. Of course, this strategy had a steep cost in Vietnam: 'Defactualization and problem-solving were welcomed because disregard of reality was inherent in the policies and goals themselves.'

Maybe we have to see a different world to make a different world. If there ever were a problem big enough for the ends solving it to justify the means, it might be climate change. Perhaps that is the well-intentioned notion behind the odd–even scheme: if people think that change is afoot, they will want to be a part of it. A little bit of over-optimism could make success look inevitable. Then, everybody will want to be on the winning side.

Psychologists call this tactic 'descriptive norms'. If you want some people to adopt a behaviour, describe it as what everybody like them does. Robert Cialdini, a social psychologist, summarized the logic: 'If everyone is doing it,' people reason, 'it must be a sensible thing to do.' Taken one step further, if you want people to do something, make them believe that everybody like them is going to do it.

Cialdini famously demonstrated his theory with an environmentally friendly example. Cialdini's team turned a parking garage into a psychology experiment. As part of the experiment, the researchers filled the parking garage with litter. When unwitting research subjects returned to their cars, 'the floor of the parking structure had been heavily littered by the experimenters with an assortment of handbills, candy wrappers, cigarette butts, and paper cups.' Half of the experimental subjects saw such trash; half of them returned to a parking garage that was spotless. The experimenters kept themselves busy by dirtying the clean garage or cleaning their litter every two hours.

When the research subjects reached their cars, they each found a flyer under the windshield wiper: 'This is automotive safety week. Please drive carefully.' The experimenters watched to see what people did with the unwanted flyers. Did they take the papers into their car, to throw away later? Or did they litter them onto the ground of the garage?

Descriptive norms made the difference. Most of the subjects who arrived to a dirty garage added their flyer to the litter. If everyone thinks it is fine to litter here, why not? But only a tiny fraction of the subjects threw their flyer into a garage that was clean. In neither case was there a convenient trash can. Behaving responsibly with the flyer meant accepting the hassle of taking it home to throw it away. But despite the hassle, humans have a tendency to conform: many would-be litterers did what they thought others were doing.

If making the garage seem clean is a way to fight litter, is making environmental policy seem effective a strategy to fight pollution? If so, we might have found our explanation for environmental pseudo-policy. The problem is, climate change is not a littered car park. It solves the wrong problem to persuade citizens that pollution is already handled. A wave of popular optimism is not going to flip the one switch that turns off a coal plant. That will be the choice of somebody in a political job. Voters may be able to influence whose job it is – but to do so, they need basic facts.

So, this explanation will not work. Arendt may have been right that leaders must sometimes lie to achieve change. But even if so, lying will not end particulate pollution. Coal plants are impervious to descriptive norms. We need another explanation for the odd–even scheme and the miniature solar plant.

The best they can do?

This chapter has considered the possibility that fake environmental policy is all part of a big plan. On this hope, the right nudges in the right places will switch everybody's sodas from plastic straws to paper ones. A grimmer possibility is that there is no big plan. Perhaps the administrative, technical, and political constraints on India's governance imply that better policies are out of India's realistic reach.

If so, that would be no criticism of the particular bureaucrats who happen to hold these jobs today: India's air pollution is a hard problem. But then, what is needed is an honest reckoning with the challenge. Capacities will not improve without investment. But, instead, policymakers who understand their limits might prefer to *appear* to be doing something, rather than admit that they are currently doing the best that they can.

Sometimes, public problems fester without resolution because nobody powerful cares whether they are ever solved. But if capacity constraints are the explanation for pretending to fight pollution, the problem would be that some people *do* care about pollution – just not the most powerful people, and not enough. Some urban voters and some media commentators do care about the air pollution, or even about climate change, and are willing to criticize the government if it ignores these issues. But India has not yet reached the point where many people are willing to change their votes over pollution. The result is a clear set of political incentives for leaders: *appear* to be doing something satisfactory, but do not be too worried if it does not actually do any good.

Part of this explanation would have to be that there is no easy
option for policymakers to actually reduce pollution. If there
were, it would be at least as effective to take that option and do
some good. So, we need to know how limited the government's
environmental policy options are. Do India's politicians have the
realistic option of technocratic environmental regulation?

The capacity of the Indian state to manage its environmental
externalities is limited in two important ways: at the top
and at the bottom. The top is where the leading guidelines
of environmental policy are researched, debated and agreed
upon: it is where the big picture is decided. The bottom is the
smokestack-level bureaucracy: where some clerk, police officer,
or other agent of the state tells a factory that its emissions are
unacceptable. Like the emission testers in Mexico City or the
local bureaucrats in China, these are the people who do or do
not make environmental policy happen.

A team of economists investigated smokestack-level
regulatory capacity in Gujarat. Esther Duflo and co-authors
studied a system where it was common knowledge that industrial
pollution often was not monitored at all. 'Although the Gujarat
High Court put in place several safeguards to limit conflicts of
interest, the basic financial arrangement underlying these audits
is typical of the practice all over the world – plants hire and pay
auditors directly, and the work of those auditors is subject to very
little oversight. In conversations we had before beginning this
study, the regulators, auditors and polluting plants all agreed that
the status quo audit system produced unreliable information.'

The economists found that the price of an entire audit was
sometimes cheaper than the price of merely measuring pollution.
These prices were clear economic evidence that pollution was
not even measured. Recall the implausible statistics reported

by the Chinese local governments. Here too, the unmistakable signature of corruption was the statistically implausible concentration of measurements exactly below the regulatory threshold. The economists found that almost one-third of plants with audits below the threshold were, in fact, too polluting.

As part of their study, the economists experimented with a system of 'back-checking' that audited the auditors. Unsurprisingly, when auditors thought that they might be audited by the research team (and potentially lose money as a result), they reported more accurate measurements.

'Who will police the police?' is one of the oldest questions in politics. A series of auditing studies by economists working in developing countries have produced usefully contradictory results. Monitoring and auditing only help if the person being monitored believes that the audit will be believed – and that reward or punishment will follow. Two similar experiments from the same district in Rajasthan demonstrated this by having different results. In one, monitoring teachers at NGO schools improved the teachers' performance. There, the NGO enforced performance pay based on monitoring. In the other, monitoring nurses at government clinics did not improve their attendance – because their government bosses excused the absences anyway.

In the case of Gujarati industry, it was the *researchers* who organized the second layer of auditing and who stood willing to enforce it with payments made or withheld (although they collaborated with the Gujarati government). Outside of a research study, whether to take audits and measurements seriously is a political question. The upshot is that smokestack-level capacity depends, in part, on policy choices at the top.

Navroz Dubash and Neha Joseph used Right to Information (RTI) requests to document how the Indian state makes high-level climate policy. They studied the few years leading up to the change of government in mid-2014. The most striking finding of their study is just how few people hold the jobs that write India's response to one of its deepest vulnerabilities. The coming and going of a Minister of Environment and Forests made a big difference to the attention paid to climate change. But even during periods of relative activity, work was accomplished through ad hoc teams, committees, and partnerships, rather than by building enduring institutions. When somebody in some part of the Indian state did turn attention to climate policy, efforts were not coordinated across departments.

Dubash and Joseph report a striking tabulation of personnel. 'Even in the core nodal agency of Ministry of Environment and Forests, full-time employees focused on climate change in the Climate Change Unit are a section officer, three scientists, a director, and a joint secretary (the latter also handling the Montreal Protocol), adding to six full-time staff.' Contrast this tiny staff with India's large economic vulnerability to climate change as documented by the World Bank; with the scope for economic benefits that, according to Nordhaus, an international climate-trade club could bring India; or with the million Indian babies that could be killed by heat and humidity from climate change at the very start of life. State Action Plans for climate change received even less serious attention. 'A limited sample of five states reveals… that relatively little institutional capacity had been created, and all the states relied heavily on donor agencies and consultants to prepare state plans.'

Strong arms and clumsy fingers

Many books before this one highlighted the weakness or incapacity of the Indian state. But it is important not to oversimplify. In fact, the Indian state is often active, making big moves: building millions of toilets, issuing bans, distributing

LPG cylinders, closing roads. In other words, the Indian state indeed has its powers: it can build things, it can ban things, and it can give things to citizens.

As with baggies in Uttar Pradesh, much of the banning is done by the courts. In 2000, the Supreme Court ruled that buses, taxis, and autorickshaws in Delhi must run on Compressed Natural Gas (CNG), rather than more polluting fuels. Here, the state proved capable: the ban was implemented and new vehicles used cleaner fuel.

For a while, it helped. But many polluting vehicles moved over borders to neighbouring states that were exempt from the rules, according to Naresh Kumar and Andrew Foster, two researchers both then at Brown University. 'The data reveals that no significant improvement in air quality has been made in the post-regulation period,' they conclude, 'alluding to the fact that the reduction in air pollution because of CNG regulations on buses, taxis and autorickshaws has been offset by a phenomenal increase in the number of private vehicles, particularly cars and non-CNG heavy vehicles.' Kumar and Foster's is not the only study of the CNG rule – but in 2019, we do not need fancy statistics to conclude that air pollution is still a problem.

The story of CNG in Delhi demonstrates the dangers of an aggressive ban – even when the ban really is enforced. A ban is a blunt tool. The state may ban the wrong things; people may work around the details of the ban; other developments may render the ban obsolete. In the meantime, enforcing the ban disrupts lives and imposes costs on citizens. Worse still, if the state's tools are clunky or imprecise, it may not be able to direct those costs towards those who can better afford them.

But even if such a ban is fruitless, it is an act of strength. So, it cannot be correct that the Indian state is simply weak. Instead it is bounded in other ways: by its size relative to the population, by its human resources, by the strength of India's enduring social forces and hierarchies. Bullying, as children know, is often a sign of another weakness: insecurity, perhaps, or anger at an inability to match the right action to the right situation.

When it bans or builds, the Indian state swings its long, powerful arms. In the process, it may do unintended damage. Meanwhile, nobody may notice that it lacks control of its fingers. Thus, part of the weakness of this Indian state is that it lacks not strength but dexterity. Such clumsiness is obscured by the contemporary image of governance as computerized public management. It is visible in the banned bags heaped next to a concrete public building.

Capacities change

So, the capacity of the Indian state is limited – if not the strength of its arms, the precision of its fingers. But the story does not end there. As we saw in the last chapter, there are administratively simple options, such as not building new coal plants. Moreover, capacity sometimes changes. In the long run, capacity can be built – and whether to do so is a political choice.

Politics can be surprising, even to experts. Political scientist Philip Tetlock tracked the political predictions of experts over twenty years. Exposed to scrutiny as statistical data, supposedly expert political judgement did little better than random guesses. In 2014, Prime Minister Narendra Modi promised to end open defecation in rural India by 2019. In 2017, when little had changed in rural sanitation, I wrote that I expected nothing much would happen. On that, I was wrong about something important.

Of course, open defecation was not eliminated. Many independent sources of survey data confirm that, as I write in late 2018, much open defecation remains in the rural plains states. Moreover, the fraction of people there who still defecate

in the open *despite* having latrines has not changed over the
last four years. But here is where I was wrong: quite a lot of
official activity *happened* and many latrines were built – in some
cases for people who did not want them. Many people were
even threatened with losing their benefits, their rations, or their
children's place in school if they did not go along with the rapid
toilet scheme. Again, the Indian state swung strong arms, not
gentle fingers. Survey data shows that the villages in north India
where more people were aware of threats were, on average, the
villages that eventually had the least open defecation.

What I misunderstood about sanitation policy a few years
ago was just how much political priority would be attached
to the prime minister's absurdly ambitious goal. I thought the
promise would be left to fizzle into the forgotten past. Instead,
the decision was taken to send open defecation out with a bang
– and to hope that nobody looked too hard through the smoke.

In the process, capacities changed. New jobs were created
and new tasks were assigned to existing roles. The focus
was latrine construction, not behaviour change. But there
was a lot of construction. Unfortunately, rural sanitation (of
all things) became a target of its own exaggerations in the
process. The government was unwilling to celebrate the honest
accomplishment of having accelerated the decline in rural open
defecation.

Instead, sanitation bureaucrats collaborated with international
development funders to engineer data that overstated success.
Asimov would have been shocked at the needless effort. Arendt,
too, would have wondered: 'Under normal circumstances the
liar is defeated by reality,' she reflected, 'even if he enlists the
help of computers.' Computers have improved since she wrote
in 1971, and are still used for this purpose.

Could a more honest and realistic approach to rural
sanitation have done more good with less harm? When October

of 2019 comes, will policymakers assume that open defecation is finished, and ignore the work left to be done? Or was the sanitation programme that rural India got the best available balance of truth and falsehood, benefits and costs? I do not know.

So, open defecation remains. Many people were coerced. Yet, open defecation probably declined more quickly than many of us 'experts' predicted. I mistakenly thought the state just did not have the capacity to issue so many combinations of toilets paired with threats. Maybe, just as surprisingly, the political will to get particles out of India's air could appear.

Being diplomatic

Because particulate pollution is not like litter – because India's citizens are more likely to be voters than industrial plant managers – we have yet to find a good rationale for officials' not levelling with the public about air pollution. If nothing else, people need to know the truth to plan around it, to raise their families. So much for any benefits of lying in domestic policy. But might Arendt have a point internationally? Could India achieve its international climate policy goals by being a little *less* straightforward?

International negotiations are often called 'diplomacy'. It is not a coincidence that the word has two meanings. To say that somebody is 'being diplomatic' is a diplomatic way of implying that they are not presenting an unsavoury truth in all its bluntness.

In international climate discussions, India's leaders have stressed the importance of differentiated responsibility. Of course, that is right: the rich countries started climate change and have the most moral responsibility to fix it. But anyone with a spouse or a friend or a co-author knows that it is not always the most useful plan to say everything that is true. Is historical responsibility a good reason for the US and Europe to decarbonize quickly and pay for the developing world's transition? Of course! Is India's best strategic response to climate injustice to emphasize this moral fact at the cost of appearing uncooperative?

Well, that depends on the consequences. In Chapter 5, we saw the results of tweaking Nordhaus's climate-economy model into a *forward-looking* model in which reducing emissions hurts poorer countries more than richer countries. Such an approach makes no explicit reference to historical responsibility (as ethically important as historical responsibility may be). And yet, it still produces the global recommendation that rich countries decarbonize quickly while leaving room for poor and emerging countries' continued development. That recommendation is rightfully India's goal.

So, India has room to present an international narrative that may appear more collaborative than the way it has framed these issues in the past. Even more important are co-benefits. Particulate pollution is so harmful that India could do only the activities that are in its near-term self-interest for human development, yet still end up being able to present itself as an international leader.

With a little bit of cheerful over-optimism – a little bit of an enthusiastic presentation of India's ambitions eventually to mitigate – the country could attempt to construct a winning team. We do not litter in this parking garage; in this climate club, we regulate our carbon emissions responsibly. Maybe, in international discussions, India could become even a little *too* optimistic about its own future emissions – after all, to change the future, Arendt reminds us, we may have to imagine things being a little different than they are.

I do not want to oversell the international benefits of over-optimism. For now, the party of Donald Trump would still be in charge of the US. Moreover, a culture of optimistic international fudging could make it harder to hold countries accountable for complying with their pledges, or with the bylaws of any trade-policy climate club. Can we be certain that 'health co-benefits domestically plus over-optimistic cooperation internationally' is India's best strategic response that we have been looking for? I cannot. But we can be certain that the odd–even driving scheme is not.

Two cheers for bureaucracy

If nobody changes their vote because of it, if the error does not strategically promote improvements, then why did the Government of India call the June 2018 air satisfactory? Why does the Delhi government stage the performance of odd–even, or the plastic bag ban? If the experts are not deceiving the voters nor deceiving the particles, then maybe the act is for other elites. After all, the electric display on Lodhi Road faces conference halls, upmarket offices, and international development agencies. Such a fancy sign may be enough for journalists, in their effort to be even-handed, to shy from accusing politicians of doing nothing.

Air pollution and climate change are technical topics. To understand the details, you have to read scientific papers and talk with scientists. To write this book, I collaborated with them. Debates are held in new scientific vocabularies. So, it is easy to overlook something or to hold incorrect beliefs – I have done both as I learned about climate policy. Experts are needed.

Many people misunderstand that environmental issues are *technical* to imply that they are *technocratic*: that to understand policymaking, we only need to talk with scientists. But one important reason why some places are more polluted than others is that governments permit externalities to continue. Too often, this fact is concealed in euphemisms like 'governance' or 'state capacity'. The euphemisms hide the reference to politics. Voters and elites could, over a long enough period of time, decide differently.

This sort of evasion is found throughout my home field of development economics. Economists like me are professionals at disguising the political with technical math. For example, it is easy to trumpet financial losses to some banks or businesses that have invested in coal. But these *private* losses should not be conflated with what economics is really about: all-things-considered efficiency and *public* well-being. The problem is not economic modelling; the problem is choosing to ask the models the wrong question. An environmental subject matter makes technical obfuscation of politics even muddier.

Indeed, environmental policymaking needs some power to be in the hands of people who are competent in the scientific details. Voters can weigh in on whether air pollution should be a higher policy priority than funding schools. Voters should not be asked how many particles of what size is the proper count. Science cannot be put to a vote.

But while understanding science is necessary, it is not enough. For starters, change begins with the political decision to empower the scientist to clean up the air in the first place. Whose interests matter most: present-day businesses, today's children, or India's future generations? That is a political question. So, environmental challenges expose the limits both of expertise and of democracy. There are inevitably two roles: for expertise and for politics.

The need for experts is one reason why fake environmental policy matters. Parents can see whether their children are learning to read or suffering from disease. Workers know how much pay they take home and how much tax they contribute. In other words, on normal issues, voters can assess how well things are going, at least for their own families. But individual voters cannot measure carbon emissions, or sort out the chemistry of source apportionment. Therefore, fake environmental policy prevents voters from fulfilling their democratic duty to hold the government accountable.

So, in this chapter, we tried to rationalize policymakers' claims to the public that particle concentrations are acceptable. We searched for an argument to justify their pretending to reduce particle pollution. We did not find one. Internationally, there may be good reason to promote global cooperation on climate policy with a little bit of careful over-optimism. But there is no such public-policy reason for the state to put on an act for its own citizens. Domestically – where what is needed is state action, not citizen coordination – the consensus-building argument for official obfuscation does not apply.

And yet, what happens is the reverse. Internationally, India has been known for forthright climate realism and willingness to blame. Domestically, meanwhile, citizens are asked to put their hopes for cleaner air in fifteen days (Sundays exempted) of the odd–even scheme. Arendt saw the same puzzle in the Pentagon Papers: 'The crucial point here is not merely that the policy of lying was hardly ever aimed at the enemy [today we might instead suggest rich, high-emitting countries], but was destined chiefly, if not exclusively, for domestic consumption, for propaganda at home, and especially for the purpose of deceiving Congress.'

The next chapter turns to India's voters. But voters cannot clear the air alone, without the leadership of India's administrative and scientific experts. Fortunately – and unlike in other countries – India's administration is led by quite smart people. Many received technical training (such as in engineering) before their public service careers. India's top bureaucrats get their jobs by taking multiple-choice tests. The winners are sent to classrooms in the mountains for even more education before taking up their administrative jobs. I have taught there, and these students are as tough a crowd as Princeton's policy school.

The experts are now tested again – and the difficult new questions of air pollution are not multiple-choice. There exists little guidance for these new challenges in the familiar templates of India's policymaking. New research is still emerging, so some answers to the test are only now reaching the textbooks. (One key reason that knowledge is delayed is that, over decades, the Indian state has done so little to measure air pollution and its causes, or to register deaths and record population health.) Still, enough is now known to take action.

Most importantly: it is not enough to pretend to answer the question and hope that the grader does not notice the fudge when marking papers. The objective facts of particle concentrations and rising temperatures will not be grading on a curve. To lead the search for solutions, bureaucrats and experts must first acknowledge the limits of expertise, and of the reach and control of the state.

8

Conclusion

Uttar Pradesh is administered from buildings near the defunct pollution display board in Hazratganj. The Indira and Jawahar Bhawans' tall towers are not the only bureaucratic office blocks in Lucknow. But they are the offices that I know best, because they are the state headquarters for rural development and for sanitation. I have spent many hours among their string-tied folders and untied wires, keeping my distance from the windows. Missing panes of glass turn the imagination towards the prospect of a nine-storey fall.

Once, on a visit to meet with sanitation staff, I was disappointed to find the men's restroom on their floor unusable. The stalls were filled with pieces of broken furniture. Through a broken window, I heard Sangita startle next door. A light bulb in the women's room exploded, showering her with sparks. If that sounds like it could catch on fire, it did. A 2016 fire on the eighth floor of Indira Bhawan 'was controlled within an hour' according to the *Times of India*. The article quoted the chief fire officer: 'Indira Bhawan lacks a proper fire protection system.' Electrical cuts in the towers trap staff in elevators. The Hindi daily *Amar Ujala* reported in 2018 that one office worker was

215

trapped in two elevators in two separate power cuts in the same day.

When research collaborators visit me in UP, I take them to Indira Bhawan on the weekend. From the ground, it looks a little like snowfall. The remaining windows are opened and piles of papers are pushed through them. This is the weekly cleaning process. Trash – in stacks, piles, and wads – is shoved through the windows and flutters to the ground, onto awnings, or wherever else it lands. Many papers – in ventilation shafts, on outcroppings, or in the motorcycle parking – remain where they fall. The offices are prepared for another week of administration and regulation.

෮

This book concludes with a few recommendations towards clearing India's air. I warned in the introduction that the book ends with open questions, not detailed instructions. But India's citizens and leaders do know enough to begin working towards solutions where they can, and building capacity where they cannot yet. This chapter considers what voters and democracy could do, while making four final recommendations along the way.

Recommendation 1: *Build towards a state that is capable of regulating air pollution.*

Pollution is a market failure. Only the government can fix it. So, the first step is to work towards state institutions with the capacity to govern pollution. These include transparent monitoring, credible data, and the ability to influence outcomes by using market prices as a policy tool.

We are all encouraged to behave environmentally: replace our light bulbs, recycle, substitute reusable metal straws for plastic ones. These may all be great ideas. Making houses and buildings more energy efficient, in particular, offers a type of co-benefit. It saves energy while making it easier to keep out particle pollution. But India's serious environmental challenges will not be solved by green-tinted exhortations that we each personally become a little bit more virtuous. Morality will not solve air pollution or climate change.

State action might. So, we can sensibly call for more environmentally ethical behaviour. But nobody should allow such calls to displace focus from the necessary role of environmental governance. And here is the problem: environmental governance needs state capacity to govern.

Opponents of environmental regulation might mistakenly welcome the weakness of the Indian state. In fact, the better state capacity to govern, the smaller the costs of any transition need to be. Recall the difference between a state with strong arms and a state with careful fingers. A low-capacity state has only one painful solution for unpaid electricity bills, open defecation, or any other problem: send the police out to harass, fine, and maybe beat people. When the police go home, everything goes back to normal.

Similarly, we saw in Chapter 5 that how aggressive climate mitigation policy should be depends on who is paying for it within each country. Clearing the air is more socially affordable if the taxes fall on the rich. It is more harmful if the sacrifice is taken from the poor. A more dextrous state can better direct the costs of a healthier environment to the citizens who can afford it.

More sophisticated governance starts with weak performance standards, which then are raised over time. As standards tighten, they only ever demand what the state can enforce. Gradually raising performance standards – ideally by using markets and prices as policy tools – improves outcomes without sudden shocks or disruptions. It is how today's rich countries arrived at fire-resistant buildings, safely packaged meat, and energy efficiency codes.

As long as standards keep improving, it is not so important if they start at low levels. The eventual goal is a price on carbon emissions that matches the social cost that extra pollution imposes on everybody. If the price of polluting becomes a little higher, then only the most productive polluting activities will continue. Such a strategy is the sensible alternative to declaring plastic bags suddenly illegal; threatening six months in jail for anyone caught in possession of polythene, and calling the problem solved. But it needs more data and more attention, sustained over a long period of time.

The problem is that it is not clear that the Indian state is yet up to the task. There are many critical unknowns in environmental policy. Nobody knows, for example, exactly by how much temperatures will rise when the concentration of CO_2 in the air is doubled. Nobody knows if countries that are spared will accept millions of international migrants. Nobody knows what the political pressure of that migration will do to social welfare policy everywhere. Among these unknowns, India's governance is a crucial but under-appreciated question. Will India develop the state capacity to regulate pollution – and do so soon enough?

China: Red, green, or blue?

The tools that can clear the air are straightforward and well-known. Independent sources of information. Objective standards of accountability. A balance of power between technical experts and political leaders. Workable, credible targets, with incentives for verifiably meeting them. All large, successful organizations use these tools. If India can build tens of millions of latrines in just a few years, it can invest in the capacity to regulate pollution using quantitative facts.

China did. Its air has improved. According to Matthew Kahn and Siqi Zheng, PM_{10} particle pollution over Beijing has fallen from about 180 in 2001 to about 100 in 2013. Kahn and Zheng explain that China's success 'hinges on central and local governments' increased willingness to tackle pollution problems'. In other words, it was a political choice. They argue that China's 'shift in government priorities is due to a desire to please urbanites'. China is not a free and fair electoral democracy. But its politics still depend, to some degree, on the collaboration of the population in the continued rule of China's elites. Its leaders realized that effectively fighting air pollution would be a popular, feasible step towards remaining in charge. China's rulers might have been motivated to achieve the support of the urban population, but in India, air pollution harms rural citizens too.

The tools that the Chinese state used to clear the air, Kahn and Zheng report, are unsurprising: 'As the price of monitoring environmental quality using remote sensing and random inspections declines [due, presumably, to technological progress], the central government can conduct more audits. If the government announces that it will heavily punish local officials who report environmental excellence while independent audits suggest a lack of environmental progress, this will provide a strong incentive for local mayors to truthfully report the current state of their city's environmental situation.'

All of this is obvious to anyone familiar with official statistics. None of it takes magic. Just the opposite – gradually strengthening standards and carbon prices would be an even better approach than China's 'heavy' punishment. Moreover, China's approach to clearing its air has not always taken advantage of co-benefits between particle pollution and greenhouse gas emissions. For example, Yue Quin and co-authors reported in 2017 that China was replacing household coal burning with synthetic natural gas (which is made from coal). This switch reduces particle pollution in the air, but also increases carbon emissions.

A darker way that India could follow China's footsteps would be to suppress discussion of problems and challenges. Environmental health requires science. Science requires free inquiry. Barbara Freese is an environmental attorney who wrote a book surveying the 'human history' of coal – from its beginnings as jewellery in the Roman Empire, through its transformative power in the industrial revolution, to the global threat that its emissions pose today.

Without Freese's awareness or consent, the Chinese translation of her book was censored to exclude the chapter on coal in China. Coal 'made China an eleventh-century superpower', Freese writes, but also darkened its skies in the 1990s. Freese discovered the censorship when her daughter bought the book in China while studying abroad.

Recall Brian Min, the political scientist who used satellite measurements of electrical lights to show that India's politicians manipulate electricity supply to win elections. The ability to redirect the flow of electricity to reward and punish voters is a remarkable form of state capacity. But the capacity to capture state resources is not the capacity we mean. It would be better if such capabilities were unused. It would be better if politicians instead paid attention to improving the electrical grid for everybody. To clear its air, India must learn from China's political commitment to meaningful responses to particle pollution – without undermining India's free democracy in the process. State capacity must come with state restraint.

Sustainable development will not happen on its own

The share of the world living in extreme poverty has fallen from 85 per cent in 1800, through 50 per cent in 1966, to only 9 per cent in 2017. That was the year before *Factfulness*, a book by Swedish statistician Hans Rosling, turned pages of graphs into a global bestseller. Rosling offers 'statistics as therapy', counselling that 'it is easy to be aware of all the bad things happening in the world. It's harder to know about the good things: billions of improvements that are never reported'. Global life expectancy has increased from thirty-one years in 1800 to seventy-two years in 2017. No country now has a life expectancy below fifty years – the level that Sweden reached at the beginning of the 20th century.

The attentive and loving care of mothers and fathers for generations of babies has driven many of these improvements. Experts debate the statistics, but it is hard to find clear and compelling evidence that development aid has done much to help, at least in the big picture. Manju made more contributions to human development than most development professors I know. Her two boys, if they lived in Sweden, would now be starting pre-kindergarten at the age of four.

Rosling's therapeutic news is that life is getting better, despite it all. You might think the improvements are because of global governance; I am inclined to instead say that they are in spite of it (with an eye towards vaccines, toilets, antibiotics, and economic growth). But we can agree that lives are improving fast. If all the development professionals threw themselves a conference tomorrow, they could celebrate that over 100,000 fewer people lived in extreme poverty than the day before. They could repeat the celebration every day.

Unfortunately, India's air and the global climate are exceptions to Rosling's trend. Air pollution and carbon emissions are not going to solve themselves while politicians celebrate. Pollution is an externality, so the invisible hand points in the wrong direction.

Some people have worried that the worsening of India's pollution means that the country faces an inevitable choice between development and the environment. We have seen that this is not the case. Pollution harms health. Suffering and illness are bad enough, but the life-long economics of human capital makes today's damage tomorrow's lasting loss. So, controlling pollution would offer economic benefits. Cleaning India's air is in its self-interest today, and in its enduring interests tomorrow.

Recommendation 2: *Co-benefits are at the core of sustainable development – India should mitigate as much as its own self-interest demands (and may then strategically achieve more internationally).*

In Chapter 5, we worried that India may have no good option in the face of climate injustice from richer countries. Now we know that co-benefits are the core of India's strategy. It was not logically necessary that India's short-term and long-term interests would align. It could have been the case that air pollution was not as bad for health as it is. It could have been the case that particle pollution's cooling effects are larger than they are. But in the real challenges that India faces, there is a policy opportunity. Policies with co-benefits address two problems at once: making India healthier, making the next generation more productive, and reducing greenhouse gas emissions.

This book has focused on the big-picture issue of electricity generation. But another opportunity for co-benefits is transportation. Many Indian families do not yet own cars. Future housing stock, where citizens of an eventually urbanized India will live, has not yet been built. In contrast, the infrastructure of the US has already been built around cars; the infrastructure of other countries has been built around public transit. When I fly from Sweden to Texas, I see families with babies lug prams in Europe and car seats in America.

India is still making that political choice, especially as cities like Kanpur grow. The Delhi Metro is rightly a source of civic pride – but anyone who has experienced its crowds knows that even the Metro is small relative to demand. Public transit is healthier, safer from accidents, more equitable, better for today's particle pollution, and better for tomorrow's climate vulnerability (if everybody agrees to organize society around it, that is; unfortunately, just you or me waiting for underfunded buses accomplishes little).

Public transit requires coordination and politics. Once I returned to Delhi to find that my friend's apartment where I had been staying had turned into the headquarters of a campaign: '*Bus ko rasta do!*' Make way for buses! One dedicated bus lane in south Delhi was eventually declared by the authorities. But it would have been the job of state enforcement to keep cars out of the 'dedicated' lane. Explicitly or implicitly, the government decided not to. So, the lane made little difference.

Once India has self-interestedly reduced air pollution (that is, just in the ways and to the extent that would make the Indian population better off), there is a further opportunity. At the next global conference, India could talk about it in a way that promotes its international interests. With blue skies, healthy lungs, and coal plants turning off, India would have a serious case to make to the international community that it is a climate policy leader. India is climate vulnerable and has much to gain from global action. As Nordhaus has computed, a climate club, enforced with international trade policy, could be one effective tactic.

India need not harm its economic and human development to get there. The co-benefits of healthy air should be more than enough to decide what to do. India wins in money and health, now and in the future, domestically and internationally, if it can construct a cooperative, trade-linked international climate club that rewards the country for the mitigation that its human capital co-benefits already demand.

Today's babies cannot vote – and neither can tomorrow's

Unfortunately, the promise of co-benefits does not altogether remove environmental policy from the political fray. India, overall, would benefit from tackling air pollution. But a few people would lose, such as investors in coal. So, politics must decide who wins and who loses.

Politics is a difficult way to improve policies – but not improving policies is worse. Even policies that would make almost everybody better-off can have political costs to actually achieve. One example is from the history of environmental policy in the US. It may seem difficult to remember now, but in 2008 the Republican and Democratic candidates for President both supported a cap-and-trade system of regulating carbon emissions. A majority of Republican and Democratic voters reported, in polls, that they believed in climate change. In those days, the larger enemy of the environment was indifference (not unified Republican opposition).

In 2009, the Democratic Party controlled the House of Representatives, the Presidency, and even a 60-vote majority in the Senate: enough to overcome a filibuster. In the fragmented US system, such concentration of power happens once in a lifetime. The Democratic Party could have enacted any legislation that it agreed on. A cap-and-trade bill, known as 'Waxman–Markey', even passed the House. But it was never seriously considered in the Senate. The moment passed.

Everybody was focused elsewhere: first on the recovery from the 2008 recession, then on the year-long struggle to improve US healthcare, to pass the legislation known as 'Obamacare'. If all the political attention of the leaders of the Democratic Party had been directed towards passing the best possible version of

Waxman–Markey, instead of passing Obamacare, it is difficult to imagine that cap-and-trade would not have passed. The US would have been pursuing serious climate policy. Maybe the 2009 Copenhagen Summit would have resulted in an agreement. Would that have been better than the good done by bringing health insurance to millions of Americans (who were disadvantaged relative to their country, but often not in global comparison)? We will never know – but it was not better according to the implicit political choice of the 2009 Democratic Party. This suggests a question: did democracy constrain the 2009 politicians to make a decision in the public interest of everybody?

If the US political system teaches us anything, it is the paradox that holding elections is not sufficient for outcomes in the public interest. Trump, Brexit, and the ongoing election of reactionary after reactionary around the world has led even sober political scientists to question what democracy is good for. Christopher Achen and Larry Bartels titled their 2016 book *Democracy for Realists*. They argue against a 'folk theory' of democracy, in which voters choose what is good for them. 'The causal chain for most important social events is complex and untraceable,' Achen and Bartels explain, so it would be a miracle if voters fully understood policy. 'Even the most attentive citizens mostly cannot figure it out.'

Achen and Bartels have in mind classic questions of political economy, such as how taxes and the money supply should be settled. Everybody recognizes that these questions need at least some expertise. That is why central banks are usually somewhat insulated from the political process. But if voters do not follow macroeconomic details, their gut feelings are even less able to handle the scientific questions of environmental policy. So, democracies need expertise (hopefully Chapter 7 has not left us too nervous about the experts).

The experts and bureaucrats are subject to the voters, if the voters choose to exercise their power. Part of Achen and Bartels' point is to document how silly voters can be. Statistics show that voters punish incumbent politicians for floods, droughts, and even shark attacks – that is, factors out of the government's control. It is enough to make one wonder *Why Bother with Elections?* as the title of a 2018 book by Adam Przeworski asks. Przeworski agrees with Achen and Bartels: the benefit of holding elections is not that they rationally respond to facts, or that they guarantee good policies. Instead, perhaps the benefit of elections is that they peacefully settle the question of who should govern. To Przeworski, the benefit of elections is 'civil peace': elections 'process whatever conflicts may arise in society in a way that maintains liberty and peace'.

Yet, even this modest benefit of democracy is undermined by climate change. Climate policy involves a conflict between the goals of a few present-day people and the well-being of many future generations. In other words, the conflict that has arisen in human society is across decades or centuries. But this conflict is not being processed by any election. If future people could vote for US Senators, Waxman–Markey would have passed.

Consider *all* of the Indian people who will be hurt by the choices that Indian politicians make about how much coal to burn in the next few years. Most of those Indians have not yet been conceived. Many of those who have been born are not yet old enough to vote – and some will never live long enough. These citizens of India's democracy are not participants in electing today's environmental policies or processing today's conflicts. For political theorists, whose job it is to identify the fundamental benefits of electoral democracy, climate change is a troubling case.

Democracy as accountability

Climate change is a problem that challenges the value of democracy. It is easy to imagine China's ruling party – focused on extending its rule by decades – being more attentive to environmental health than an electoral democracy where all eyes are on the next quarter's stock market returns, or on the allegedly disagreeable properties of a disadvantaged out-group. Understanding that most Indians who have a stake in environmental policy are excluded from elections (because they are not yet alive) should change how we understand democracy. So should the fact that so many who are alive to face risks today do not understand them. But these do not add up to an argument to do away with democracy, especially not without a proposal of who else to put in charge. It is a reminder that the extent of who counts in policymaking does not go far enough. It is also a reminder that elections are only one part of what makes democracy important. Another pillar of democracy is the accountability of the government to the public – and to independent sources of information.

Recommendation 3: *Citizens and civil society organizations must take up the government's neglected duty to measure air pollution.*

You cannot clean your own air, but you can measure it. Air pollution monitors are not so expensive. My small research team has owned several of them. We dropped one onto a tiled floor. Josh Apte puts them in autos for his research. Some of my richer friends in Delhi now have them in their houses. As long as the government is not adequately measuring air pollution, setting up your own air quality monitor is an act of citizenship. The next step is to collate the data in the hands of citizens and make it available to everyone online.

This work is already underway. According to the *New York Times*, in December 2018, personal air quality monitors are 'the hot Silicon Valley gift this holiday season'. As the reporter did not resist observing, 'the idea of buying a personal pollution monitor because you don't trust the government sounds like the most Bay Area techie thing ever'. But, in protecting themselves, citizens can protect others, too – if the data is shared and organized. Google Maps knows about traffic because it collects data from everybody's phones and processes it. Aggregating private monitors would not be a complete substitute for adequate public monitoring of air pollution because personal monitors only measure the *level* of air pollution. They would not register the details necessary to compute its *sources*. Still, decentralized data collection could enable coordinated accountability for pollution policies.

If the Indian state is not going to measure air pollution, then India's many distinguished civil society organizations can. India has a long tradition of action research. The Annual Status of Education Report (ASER) survey has tracked child reading and math outcomes throughout India for years. Their data are independently collected and available online. Social programmes such as NREGA or the public distribution of food have always been imperfectly implemented; dialogue with independent organizations reports the facts from the field and holds governments accountable for doing better. In the best cases, information from committed citizen organizations has been a tool that the government uses to improve.

Not all cases are the best cases, unfortunately. Too often, governments are not interested in independent information or dissenting data. Sometimes, the Government of India has threatened organizations that plan to collect or distribute statistics that challenge official claims. Civil society organizations have a crucial democratic purpose in those cases too: to offer citizens information and an unofficial take on the quantitative facts. Along the way, civil society can strengthen democracy in another way: by highlighting the interests of future Indians who are not yet here to vote.

Many voters, newspaper reporters, and op-ed columnists have a rough sense of what inflation, unemployment or GDP growth numbers entail. They can learn to understand what a $PM_{2.5}$ of 400 means too. Organizations that can work towards such public understanding need resources and time. Tweeting about a polluted day helps – but 140 characters is no substitute for an organization developing independent expertise through years of public engagement with an issue. Already, several important organizations have long taken up this task.

Sometimes, fulfilling this purpose requires commitment. It would be a dark day for democracy if officials used the powers of the state to harass an organization for documenting a dark day for air pollution. But such a day may come. Whether in partnership with elected governments or as a contribution to democratic accountability, air pollution is too important to not be tracked, discussed, and debated by independent citizen teams.

Coal is not the future of India

Recommendation 4: *Phase out existing coal plants; do not build new ones.*

Coal is not only a fuel for India's economy: it has long been a source of power in Indian politics too. Many of India's politicians have ties to coal. The 2012 coal allocation scam drew attention throughout India and around the world. Citizen activism – including from some of India's poorest Adivasi communities – has risen as one of the few battles slowing the multiplication of coal mines and furnaces.

Political realism says that coal will still be important in India for years to come. And yet, coal plant construction responds to election outcomes. So, just because burning coal is *political* does not mean that it is *inevitable*. Precise, skilful governance is not needed to burn a lot of coal – or to stop burning it. The Indian state cannot yet prevent electricity theft or ensure that its employees in schools and clinics turn up at work. But despite these limits to state capacity, it can decide how many coal plants it builds and continues to operate.

Meanwhile, the economics of coal is changing quickly. The cost of generating an extra kilowatt-hour of electricity from renewables is falling fast. The trends suggest that it will soon be unprofitable to buy electricity from coal rather than from renewables, even at a coal plant that already exists. Combining those financial considerations with the harm done to everybody's health and human capital by burning coal yields a clear conclusion. Public investment in new or expanded coal plants does not make economic sense. Coal is already a bad economic bet and the trends are getting worse.

The good news is that economic development and environmental health are not enemies. To the contrary: the basic lessons of public economics are the core of the argument against coal and its externality harms. In fact, coal usage is declining around the world because of economics. In the US, coal is losing its economic competition with natural gas, due to fracking. In India, health co-benefits tip the economic balance away from public investment in coal. The opportunity to reduce carbon emissions and work towards international climate collaboration are further benefits for climate-vulnerable India. But numbers show that particle pollution, more than even carbon emissions, is what makes the decisive difference.

The only unknown is whether India's governance will be able to respond to the economic rationality behind these facts.

One way that governance could fail is if the interests of the few businesses, banks, and politicians who personally profit from coal, its financing, and its pollution are allowed to outweigh the interests of the population of India as a whole – old, young and yet-to-be born.

Another way that governance could fail is if changes are blunt and costly, rather than well-managed. Transitioning out of coal will incur financial and social costs – just as demonetization did, just as the taxes that pay for schools do. But India's leaders decided that the benefits of demonetization, education and other public investments outweigh the costs. With each passing winter's pollution, voters across India are learning that clearing the air does too.

In mid-2018, the sky over the Kanpur coal plant is bluer than grey. The power station is out of service. The houses outside the coal plant are being demolished. In 35°C weather with a humidity of 60 per cent, workers in dhotis and plastic sandals are destroying the neighbourhood with sledgehammers.

A few years ago, when I first visited Panki, a teenager living in one house shared his popcorn with me. A man living in another compared the ageing power plant to his old motorcycle. Both of those houses are gone now. What was a community of homes is now a field of broken bricks. The demolition work in progress has swept from south to north. At the south end, close to the market, much of the desirable pieces of brick have been cleared out – only the less useful bits remain on the ground. Further north, the salvageable bricks stand stacked into pillars that tractors haul away. A truck full of old metal door frames rumbles past the only structures left: a temple and the broken oval of the former water tower, smashed into the ground like a crashed spaceship.

The houses are being cleared away to make room for an expansion of the government's coal plant. A proposal to expand the plant had been rejected before on account of pollution. But the idea was resumed after a 2017 state election transferred power: whether to invest in coal is an economic question decided by politics. 'The UP government is planning a power-packed start to the New Year,' the *Times of India* reported on New Year's Day 2018, 'by deciding to gift a brand-new super-critical 660 MW power unit at Panki in Kanpur to citizens of the state.'

The government-commissioned Environmental Impact Assessment waives away the harm to residents: 'The nearest major town is Kanpur, which is approximately [16] km' away. In fact, the city extends continuously to and past the plant. Three million people live in Kanpur, which the WHO believes is already the world's most polluted city. The district hospital, Z-Square Mall, and Cawnpore Kotwali are all within a 13-km drive of the coal plant. A distance of 15.7 km is enough to cross the Ganga, having left Kanpur towards Lucknow.

At 660 MW, the government's new coal-burning capacity in Kanpur will be slightly larger than a new, privately constructed solar plant in Tamil Nadu. The BBC celebrated the solar plant in a recent article as 'huge', 'big' and 'humongous'. The BBC did not report on Kanpur's renewed coal plant. The panels of the solar plant in Tamil Nadu cover ten square kilometres. Solar-powered robots keep them sunny and clean. The electricity is estimated to be enough for almost half of the population of an average Indian district.

India will need hundreds of such huge solar plants to meet its needs – or more. Instead, over the five years from 2017 to 2022, projects planned or started in India would expand coal-fired capacity by about seventy-five times as much as that big solar plant. The big solar plant is a start to an alternative, but only a start. One down, seventy-four to go.

Progress will be measured in such numbers. Many of the uncertain quantities are as political as they are scientific. What concentration of $PM_{2.5}$ will children breathe in Delhi? Or in rural Uttar Pradesh's villages? How many will the smoke kill? By how much will it stunt the survivors' growth? How much particle pollution and carbon emissions will the new Kanpur coal plant put into the air? How many newspaper articles will celebrate a solar plant that is tiny, relative to the size of the challenge? How many citizens will buy their own air quality monitors?

How much lower will research push the price of renewables? How much investment in renewable energy will be stacked against increasing demand for electricity? How long will India take to pursue everyone's economic well-being, rather than coal-fired investment returns? Nobody knows the answers to these questions.

How many voters will insist on clearing the air?

Notes

Methods

In reporting qualitative evidence from field research, I have changed identifiable names of interviewees and certain local places for anonymity, attempting to preserve what is implied about social status, demographic categories, and geography. All such persons, places and events refer to a specific individual or instance: no narrative composites are used.

Some important data sources are drawn upon throughout the book:

Qualitative field research. Since mid-2011, I have spent much time living and working in Uttar Pradesh, including several years when Sitapur district was my main home. I have been visiting Kanpur periodically for reporting for this book since mid-2016. Many of the interviews in this book were done with and through the invaluable partnership of Nikhil Srivastav, my colleague at r.i.c.e.

DHS. Whenever I refer to DHS data or to undifferentiated 'demographic surveys', I mean the Demographic and Health

Surveys, known in India as the National Family Health Survey (NFHS). It is publicly available at www.measuredhs.com.

IHDS. I report some summary statistics from the India Human Development Survey (IHDS). The IHDS is a nationally representative panel of approximately 40,000 households collected in 2005 and 2012 in a collaboration between NCAER and the University of Maryland, under Principal Investigators Sonalde Desai and Reeve Vanneman. It is publicly available at ihds.info.

RICE and DICE models. All Integrated Assessment Model results represent versions or modifications of the DICE (Dynamic Integrated Climate-Economy) or RICE (Regional Integrated Climate-Economy) models, originally designed by William Nordhaus. The RICE model is publicly available at Nordhaus's website. This work has been in collaboration with Princeton's Climate Futures Initiative, led by Marc Fleurbaey (from whom I have learnt especially much), Melissa Lane and Robert Socolow.

Nordhaus, W.D., 2013. *The Climate Casino: Risk, Uncertainty, and Economics for a Warming World*. Yale University Press.

Nordhaus, W., 2018. Evolution of modeling of the economics of global warming: changes in the DICE model, 1992–2017. *Climatic Change*, Vol. 148, No. 4, pp. 623–640.

In our team's later projects, David Anthoff and Frank Errickson independently replicated our qualitative results in FUND, another IAM.

On units. $PM_{2.5}$ and PM_{10} are each sizes of fine particulate 2.5 and 10 micrometres (μm) or less respectively. Throughout this book, I report particulate pollution in units of micrograms per cubic meter, which is standard in this literature (μg/m^3). One exception is the results of the filter experiment in Chapter 1, using a Dylos 1700 laser particle counter, which reports number concentration, rather than mass (which is why that discussion did not use numerical results). I adopt a convention of typically omitting units, as in 'PM$_{2.5}$ is 460 in my bedroom!' Although this does not match usage in scientific papers, I find that it does capture popular, conversational usage among elites in Delhi.

Many of the notes below are full citations to works or authors mentioned in the text. In cases where I am elaborating on a point in the text, or where the text did not mention the name of the author, the following references provide the page number and a few words from the text in **boldface** to help the reader match the note.

Introduction

p. 1: colour coded green. Ambient Air Quality Data of Delhi Stations for the Month of June, 2018. Central Pollution Control Board.

p. 1: in the UK, US. "Daily Air Quality Index". Air UK Website. Defra.

Revised Air Quality Standards For Particle Pollution And Updates To The Air Quality Index. North Carolina: US EPA Office of Air Quality Planning and Standards. 2013.

p. 1: 36 are in Delhi. Station List of CAAQMS (Contains subsequent monitor counts, as well). See also urban emissions. info tweet: '# of PM$_{2.5}$ monitors operational = 134 in 17 states as of November, 2018. Source @ http//cpcb.nic.in'

p. 4: chemical reactions. Behera, S.N. and Sharma, M., 2010. Reconstructing primary and secondary components of PM$_{2.5}$ composition for an urban atmosphere. *Aerosol Science and Technology*, 44(11), pp. 983–992.

Apte, J.S., Kirchstetter, T.W., Reich, A.H., Deshpande, S.J., Kaushik, G., Chel, A., Marshall, J.D. and Nazaroff, W.W., 2011. Concentrations of fine, ultrafine, and black carbon particles in auto-rickshaws in New Delhi, India. *Atmospheric Environment*, Vol. 45, No. 26, pp. 4470–4480.

Daigle, Katy. Rickshaw research reveals extreme Delhi pollution. *Associated* Press. November 26, 2014.

Krzyzanowski, M., Apte, J.S., Bonjour, S.P., Brauer, M., Cohen, A.J. and Prüss-Ustun, A.M., 2014. Air pollution in the mega-cities. *Current Environmental Health Reports*, Vol. 1, No. 3, pp. 185–191.

Figure 1. Author's computation from the WHO Global Ambient Air Quality Database, 2016 data. The horizontal axis is GNI per capita, Atlas method, for 2016, from the World Bank World Development Indicators. Population size is from the UN World Population Prospects.

Dasgupta, Neha. 2018. With world's worst air, Kanpur struggles to track pollution. Reuters. 15 May.

p. 13: level of 173. [no author] 2018. India tops world in bad air quality: Kanpur, Delhi among 15 worst cities, Mumbai 4th most polluted megacity. *Times of India*. 2 May.

Figure 2. Author's computation from Spears, Dey, *et al.* data.

Figure 3. Author's computation from data available at urbanemissons.info: 'hourly averages of data from all public continuous monitoring stations' is the description given on that website, which takes data from the Delhi Pollution Control Committee.

Pant, P., Guttikunda, S.K. and Peltier, R.E., 2016. Exposure to particulate matter in India: A synthesis of findings and future directions. *Environmental research*, 147, pp. 480–496.

Deaton, A., 2013. *The Great Escape: Health, Wealth, and the Origins of Inequality*. Princeton University Press.

p. 19: poverty reduction MDG. The point here is that the 'halving' goal would have been met by pre-existing trends. Clemens, et al show this, although they concentrate on other dimensions of the MDGs, and also consider goals within countries. Clemens, M.A., Kenny, C.J. and Moss, T.J., 2007. The trouble with the MDGs: confronting expectations of aid and development success. *World Development*, Vol. 35, No. 5, pp. 735–751. For a more detailed accounting including breakdowns by region and goal (here, I only refer to the poverty reduction goal), see: Ahimbisibwe, I. and Ram, R., 2019. The contribution of Millennium Development Goals towards improvement in major development indicators, 1990–2015. *Applied Economics*, Vol. 51, No. 2, pp. 170–180.

Dasgupta, P., 2007. The idea of sustainable development. *Sustainability Science*, Vol. 2, No. 1, pp. 5–11.

Greenstone, M. and Jack, B.K., 2015. Envirodevonomics: A research agenda for an emerging field. *Journal of Economic Literature*, Vol. 53, No. 1, pp. 5–42.

p. 32: they had sure better. Broome, J., 2016. Do not ask for morality. *The Ethical Underpinnings of Climate Economics*, pp. 21–33, Routledge.

Chapter 1: Health Outside Hospitals

This chapter is based on the following two papers:

Spears, D., Dey, S., Chowdhury, S., Vyas, S., and Apte, J.S. 2018. Direct evidence of the impact of early-life exposure to ambient $PM_{2.5}$ air pollution on later-childhood height-for-age in India. Working paper presented at Population Association of America annual meetings, 2019. UT Austin and IIT Delhi.

Vyas, S., Srivastav, N. and Spears, D., 2016. An Experiment with Air Purifiers in Delhi during Winter 2015-2016. *PloS one*, Vol. 11, No. 12, p. e0167999.

Other notes:

p. 38: actual randomized experiments. Deaton, A. and Cartwright, N., 2018. Understanding and misunderstanding randomized controlled trials. *Social Science & Medicine*, Vol 210, pp. 2–21.

p. 38: one-third more. In fact, 1.35 times... 1.54 times. Mikati, I., Benson, A.F., Luben, T.J., Sacks, J.D. and Richmond-Bryant, J., 2018. Disparities in distribution of particulate matter emission sources by race and poverty status. *American Journal of Public Health*, Vol. 108, No. 4, pp.480–485.

Currie, J. and Walker, R., 2011. Traffic congestion and infant health: Evidence from E-ZPass. *American Economic Journal: Applied Economics*, Vol. 3, No. 1, pp. 65–90.

Arceo, E., Hanna, R. and Oliva, P., 2016. Does the effect of pollution on infant mortality differ between developing and developed countries? Evidence from Mexico City. *Economic Journal*, Vol. 126, No. 591, pp. 257–280.

Schlenker, W. and Walker, W.R., 2015. Airports, air pollution, and contemporaneous health. *Review of Economic Studies*, Vol. 83, No. 2, pp. 768–809.

The *Lancet* Commission on pollution and health. Vol. 391, No. 10119, pp. 462–512, 3 February, 2018. The 'two tabulations' were one by the World Health Organization and one by the Global Burden of Disease project.

Srivastav, N. 2016. Life and Death in the Real India. *Outlook*.

Dey, S., Di Girolamo, L., van Donkelaar, A., Tripathi, S.N., Gupta, T. and Mohan, M., 2012. Variability of outdoor fine particulate ($PM_{2.5}$) concentration in the Indian Subcontinent: A remote sensing approach. *Remote Sensing of Environment*, No. 127, pp. 153–161.

Kumar, N., Chu, A. and Foster, A., 2007. An empirical relationship between $PM_{2.5}$ and aerosol optical depth in

Delhi Metropolitan. *Atmospheric Environment*, Vol. 41, No. 21, pp. 4492–4503.

p. 46: correlationship. Vyas, S., 2017. Seeing through Smoke. *Caravan*.

p. 47: Monitoring of Vital Events. Setel, P.W., *et al* and Monitoring of Vital Events (MoVE) writing group, 2007. A scandal of invisibility: making everyone count by counting everyone. *The Lancet*, Vol. 370, No. 9598, pp.1569–1577.

Bozzoli, C., Deaton, A. and Quintana–Domeque, C., 2009. Adult height and childhood disease. *Demography*, Vol. 46, No. 4, pp. 647–669.

Figures 4–6. Adapted with permission from Spears, Dey, et al.

Pope III, C.A., Cropper, M., Coggins, J. and Cohen, A., 2015. Health benefits of air pollution abatement policy: role of the shape of the concentration–response function. *Journal of the Air & Waste Management Association*, Vol. 65, No. 5, pp. 516–522.

Marshall, J.D., Apte, J.S., Coggins, J.S. and Goodkind, A.L., 2015. Blue Skies Bluer?. *Environmental Science & Technology*, Vol 49, No. 24, pp. 13929–13936.

Figure 7. Drawn by author. See Pope, et al. (2015), Marshall, et al. (2015).

Kalra, A., 2018. Faced with Delhi's pollution, India's federal agencies bought air purifiers. Reuters. 20 March.

p. 65: poll of leading economics professors. IGM Economic Experts Panel. Chicago Booth Initiative of Global Markets.

Rao, K.S., 2017. *Do We Care? India's Health System*. Oxford.

Chapter 2: Fields and Villages

p. 68: regional officer. Vyas, S., 2017. Seeing through Smoke. *Caravan*.

Urbanisation on the rise in India. The *Hindu*. 18 May 2018.

Munshi, K. and Rosenzweig, M., 2016. Networks and misallocation: Insurance, migration, and the rural–urban wage gap. *American Economic Review*, Vol. 106, No. 1, pp. 46–98.

p. 70: no different for rural and urban children. In the fixed effects regression from the paper in Chapter 1 with Sagnik Dey, splitting the sample by rural and urban (or introducing an interaction) does not find a different coefficient on $PM_{2.5}$ predicting child height.

Guttikunda, S., 2011. Using top-down and bottom-up source apportionment studies to evaluate benefits and co-benefits. urbanemissions.info.

Guttikunda, S.K., Goel, R. and Pant, P., 2014. Nature of air pollution, emission sources, and management in the Indian cities. *Atmospheric Environment*, Vol. 95, pp. 501–510.

Pant, P., Shukla, A., Kohl, S.D., Chow, J.C., Watson, J.G. and Harrison, R.M., 2015. Characterization of ambient $PM_{2.5}$ at a pollution hotspot in New Delhi, India and inference of sources. *Atmospheric Environment*, Vol. 109, pp. 178–189.

Vasudeva V., 2017. Punjab farmers defy ban on stubble burning. The *Hindu*.

Khan, T. and Kishore, A. 2018. Why farmers burn the crop residue: Can't we pay or subsidize more to our farmers not to burn it? IFPRI working paper and conference poster.

Chakrabarti, S., Khan, M.T., Kishore, A., Roy, D., and Scott, S.P., 2018. Risk of acute respiratory infection from crop burning in India: estimating disease burden and economic welfare from satellite and national health survey data for 250,000 persons. working paper.

Gupta, R. and Somanathan, E. Happy Seeder: A solution to agricultural fires in north India. Ideas for India. 12 November 2016.

Rangel, M. and Vogl, T., 2019. Agricultural Fires and Health at Birth. *Review of Economics and Statistics*. forthcoming.

Currie, J., Graff Zivin, J., Mullins, J., and Neidell, M., 2014. What Do We Know About Short-and Long-Term Effects of Early-Life Exposure to Pollution?, *Annual Review of Resource Economics*.

Black, S.E., Devereux, P.J. and Salvanes, K.G., 2007. From the cradle to the labor market? The effect of birth weight on adult outcomes. *Quarterly Journal of Economics*, Vol. 122, No. 1, pp. 409–439.

Costa, D.L., 1998. Unequal at birth: A long-term comparison of income and birth weight. *Journal of Economic History*, Vol. 58, No. 4, pp. 987–1009.

p. 89: replacement of human bodies. If you have read Cowen's 2018 book *Stubborn Attachments*, I suggest that the intergenerational effects of early-life health are among Frank Knight's Crusonia plants.

Chapter 3: Homes and Kitchens

This chapter is based on the following two papers:

Gupta, A. Where There Is Smoke: Gender, Neighborhood Externalities, and Adult Respiratory Health in India. Working paper presented at Population Association of America annual meetings, 2018. Penn PSC.

Kishore, A. and Spears, D., 2014. Having a son promotes clean cooking fuel use in urban India: Women's status and son preference. *Economic Development and Cultural Change*, Vol. 62, No. 4, pp. 673–699.

Other notes:

Thompson, L.M., Bruce, N., Eskenazi, B., Diaz, A., Pope, D. and Smith, K.R., 2011. Impact of reduced maternal exposures to wood smoke from an introduced chimney stove on newborn birth weight in rural Guatemala. *Environmental Health Perspectives*, Vol. 119, No. 10, p. 1489.

Pokhrel, A.K., Bates, M.N., Verma, S.C., Joshi, H.S., Sreeramareddy, C.T. and Smith, K.R., 2009. Tuberculosis and indoor biomass and kerosene use in Nepal: A case–control study. *Environmental Health Perspectives*, Vol. 118, No. 4, pp. 558–564.

Mishra, V., Dai, X., Smith, K.R., and Mika., L., 2004. Maternal Exposure to Biomass Smoke and Reduced Birth Weight in Zimbabwe. East-West Center Population and Health Series, No. 114.

Figure 8. Adapted with permission from Gupta. (2018, PAA).

Hanna, R., Duflo, E. and Greenstone, M., 2016. Up in smoke: The influence of household behaviour on the long-run impact of improved cooking stoves. *American Economic Journal: Economic Policy*, Vol. 8, No. 1, pp. 80–114.

Hanna, R. and Oliva, P., 2015. Moving up the energy ladder: the effect of an increase in economic well-being on the fuel consumption choices of the poor in India. *American Economic Review* papers & proceedings, Vol. 105, No. 5, pp. 242–46.

Jeffery, P., Jeffery, R. and Lyon, A., 1989. *Labour pains and labour power: women and childbearing in India*. Zed.

Gupta, M.D., 1995. Life course perspectives on women's autonomy and health outcomes. *American Anthropologist*, Vol. 97, No. 3, pp. 481–491.

Chapter 4: Electricity and Economics

p. 107: Indira Gandhi. The source of the Indira Gandhi facts and the Borlaug quote is: Ramesh, J., 2017. *Indira Gandhi: A Life in Nature*. Simon & Schuster.

p. 108: cost of something. I am not sure of the origin of this phrase. I know it as part of the definition of opportunity cost in Mankiw's undergraduate textbook, but Mike of Chapter 5's wet bulb paper once found it in a fortune cookie.

Dinkelman, T., 2011. The effects of rural electrification on employment: New evidence from South Africa. *American Economic Review*, Vol. 101, No. 7, pp. 3078–3108.

Lee, K., Miguel, E., and Wolfram, C., 2018. Experimental Evidence on the Economics of Rural Electrification. Working paper UC Berkeley.

p. 112: air conditioning. Barreca, A., Clay, K., Deschenes, O., Greenstone, M. and Shapiro, J.S., 2016. Adapting to climate change: The remarkable decline in the US temperature-mortality relationship over the twentieth century. *Journal of Political Economy*, Vol. 124, No. 1, pp. 105–159.

p. 113: losses almost halved. P.M. Upreti. 2017. I have the power. *The Hindu BusinessLine*. 6 October.

Figure 9. United Nations Population Division. World Population Prospects: 2017 Revision, as reported in World Bank World Development Indicators.

Gazetteer of India. Uttar Pradesh. District Kanpur. 1989.

Lam, D., 2011. How the world survived the population bomb: Lessons from 50 years of extraordinary demographic history. *Demography*, Vol. 48, No. 4, pp. 1231–1262.

Coffey, D. and Spears, D. 2017. *Where India Goes: Abandoned Toilets, Stunted Development, and the Costs of Caste*. HarperCollins.

Ghosh, A., Gupta, A. and Spears, D., 2014. Are Children in West Bengal Shorter Than Children in Bangladesh?, *Economic & Political Weekly*, Vol. 48.

Coffey, D., 2015. Prepregnancy body mass and weight gain during pregnancy in India and sub-Saharan Africa. *PNAS*, p.201416964.

Min, B., 2015. *Power and the vote: Elections and electricity in the developing world*. Cambridge University Press.

Dubash, N.K., Kale, S., and Bharbirkar, R. eds., 2018. *Mapping Power: The Political Economy of Electricity in India's States.* Oxford University Press.

Chakravarty, S. and Tavoni, M., 2013. Energy poverty alleviation and climate change mitigation: Is there a trade off?, *Energy Economics*, Vol. 40, pp. S67–S73.

Chapter 5: Heat and Humidity

This chapter is based on the following two papers:

Geruso, M. and Spears, D., 2018. Heat, Humidity, and Infant Mortality in the Developing World. IZA Discussion Paper 11717.

LoPalo, M., Kuruc, K., Budolfson, M., and Spears, D., 2018. Quantifying India's Climate Vulnerability. *India Policy Forum*. NCAER.

Other notes:

p. 132: 19 per cent. NFHS-4. 32 per cent of Churu interviews were conducted in February 2016, the rest in March 2016.

Fu, S.H., Gasparrini, A., Rodriguez, P.S. and Jha, P., 2018. Mortality attributable to hot and cold ambient temperatures in India: a nationally representative case-crossover study. *PLoS Medicine*, Vol. 15, No. 7, p. e1002619.

Figure 10. Adapted with permission from LoPalo, *et al* (2018, *India Policy Forum*). The computation subtracts projected change in the infant mortality rate under Representative Concentration Pathway (RCP) 2.6 from our projection under RCP 8.5.

p. 144: about a million more infants will die. Averaged over India, the difference is on the order of one infant death per 1000 live births. The UN World Population Prospects project

that there will be about 100 million births in each of the
ten five-year intervals from 2050–2100. This computation
assumes no endogenous effect on fertility.

LoPalo, M., 2018. Temperature, Worker Productivity, and
Adaptation: Evidence from Survey Data Production.
working paper, UT Austin.

Mani, M., *et al.*, 2018. *South Asia's Hotspots: The Impact of
Temperature and Precipitation Changes on Living Standards.*
World Bank Group.

Coffey, D., Hathi, P., Khurana, N. and Thorat, A., 2018. Explicit
Prejudice: Evidence from a New Survey. *Economic & Political
Weekly*, Vol. 53, No. 1, p. 46–54.

Spears, D., Hathi, P., and Coffey, D. 2018., Willingness to
sacrifice for climate mitigation in representative samples of
Indian adults. UT Austin working paper.

Chakravarty, S., Chikkatur, A., De Coninck, H., Pacala, S.,
Socolow, R. and Tavoni, M., 2009. Sharing global CO_2
emission reductions among one billion high emitters.
Proceedings of the National Academy of Sciences.

Nordhaus, W.D., 2011. Estimates of the social cost of carbon:
background and results from the RICE–2011 model.
National Bureau of Economic Research working paper No.
w17540.

Nordhaus, W.D., 2017. Revisiting the social cost of carbon.
Proceedings of the National Academy of Sciences, p.201609244.

Spears, D. 2018. Nobel laureate William Nordhaus' ideas for
India. *Ideas for India.*

Budolfson, M., Dennig, F., Fleurbaey, M., Scovronick, N.,
Siebert, A., Spears, D. and Wagner, F., 2017. Optimal climate
policy and the future of world economic development. The
World Bank Economic Review.

Dennig, F., Budolfson, M.B., Fleurbaey, M., Siebert, A. and
Socolow, R.H., 2015. Inequality, climate impacts on the

future poor, and carbon prices. *Proceedings of the National Academy of Sciences*, Vol. 112, No. 52, pp. 15827–15832.

Scovronick, N., Budolfson, M.B., Dennig, F., Fleurbaey, M., Siebert, A., Socolow, R.H., Spears, D. and Wagner, F., 2017. Impact of population growth and population ethics on climate change mitigation policy. *Proceedings of the National Academy of Sciences*, Vol. 114, No. 46, pp. 12338–12343.

Nordhaus, W., 2015. Climate clubs: Overcoming free-riding in international climate policy. *American Economic Review*, Vol. 105, No. 4, pp. 1339–70.

Chapter 6: Co-benefits and Coal

This chapter is based on the following three papers:

Scovronick, N., Budolfson, M., Dennig, F., Errickson, F., Fleurbaey, M., Peng, W., Socolow, R.H., Spears, D., and Wagner, F., 2019. The impact of human health co-benefits on evaluations of global climate policy. *Nature Communications*.

Gupta, A. and Spears, D., 2017. Health externalities of India's expansion of coal plants: Evidence from a national panel of 40,000 households. *Journal of Environmental Economics and Management*, 86, pp. 262–276.

Scovronick, N, ... Spears, D., et al. 2019. Human health and the social cost of carbon: a primer and call to action. *Epidemiology*.

Other notes:

Train revenue statistics depend on the year: http://www. indianrailways.gov.in/railwayboard/uploads/directorate/ stat_econ/IRSP_2016-17/Facts_Figure/Fact_Figures%20 English%202016-17.pdf

Guttikunda, S.K. and Jawahar, P., 2014. Atmospheric emissions and pollution from the coal-fired thermal power plants in India. *Atmospheric Environment*, 92, pp.449–460.

The black hole of coal. *The Economist*. 4 August 2018.

BP Statistical Review of World Energy. 67th edition. June 2018.

Bhattacharjee, S., 2017. *India's Coal Story: From Damodar to Zambezi*. SAGE Publishing India.

p. 167: link in the causal chain.

Chowdhury, Z., Zheng, M., Schauer, J.J., Sheesley, R.J., Salmon, L.G., Cass, G.R. and Russell, A.G., 2007. Speciation of ambient fine organic carbon particles and source apportionment of $PM_{2.5}$ in Indian cities. *Journal of Geophysical Research: Atmospheres*, Vol. 112, No. D15. ('On average, primary emissions from fossil fuel combustion [coal, diesel, and gasoline] are responsible for about 25–33 per cent of $PM_{2.5}$ mass in Delhi, 21–36 per cent in Mumbai, 37–57 per cent in Kolkata, and 28 per cent in Chandigarh.')

Nagar, P.K., Singh, D., Sharma, M., Kumar, A., Aneja, V.P., George, M.P., Agarwal, N. and Shukla, S.P., 2017. Characterization of $PM_{2.5}$ in Delhi: role and impact of secondary aerosol, burning of biomass, and municipal solid waste and crustal matter. *Environmental Science and Pollution Research*, Vol. 24, No. 32, pp. 25179–25189.

Yang, M. and Chou, S.Y., 2015. Impacts of being downwind of a coal-fired power plant on infant health at birth: Evidence from the precedent-setting Portland rule. National Bureau of Economic Research working paper No. w21723.

Dubash, N.K., 2013. The politics of climate change in India: narratives of equity and cobenefits. *WIREs: Climate Change*, Vol. 4, No. 3, pp. 191–201.

Dubash, N., Raghunandan, D., Sant, G. and Sreenivas, A., 2013. Indian climate change policy: Exploring a Co-Benefits

Based approach. *Economic and Political Weekly*, Vol. 48, No. 22, pp. 47–62.

Parry, I., Veung, C., and Heini, D., 2014. How much carbon pricing is in countries' own interests? The critical role of co-benefits. IMF Working Paper WP/14/174. See also: Parry, I., 2014. Carbon Pricing: Good for you, Good for the Planet. IMF Blog.

Chowdhury, S., Dey, S. and Smith, K.R., 2018. Ambient $PM_{2.5}$ exposure and expected premature mortality to 2100 in India under climate change scenarios. *Nature Communications*, Vol. 9, No. 1, p. 318.

Watts, N., Amann, M., Arnell, N., Ayeb-Karlsson, S., Belesova, K., Berry, H., Bouley, T., Boykoff, M., Byass, P., Cai, W. and Campbell-Lendrum, D., 2018. The 2018 report of the Lancet Countdown on health and climate change: shaping the health of nations for centuries to come. *The Lancet*.

Scovronick, N. and Armstrong, B., 2012. The impact of housing type on temperature-related mortality in South Africa, 1996–2015. *Environmental Research*, Vol. 113, pp. 46–51.

p. 179: London smog. Clay, K. and Troesken, W., 2010. Did Frederick Brodie Discover the World's First Environmental Kuznets Curve? Coal Smoke and the Rise and Fall of the London Fog. National Bureau of Economic Research. Working paper No. w15669.

Sugathan, A., Bhangale, R., Kansal, V. and Hulke, U., 2018. How can Indian power plants cost-effectively meet the new sulfur emission standards? Policy evaluation using marginal abatement cost-curves. *Energy Policy*, Vol. 121, pp. 124–137.

Tong, D., Zhang, Q., Davis, S.J., Liu, F., Zheng, B., Geng, G., Xue, T., Li, M., Hong, C., Lu, Z. and Streets, D.G., 2018. Targeted emission reductions from global super-polluting power plant units. *Nature Sustainability*, Vol. 1, No. 1, p. 59.

p. 185: killing thirty-two people. Different news articles give different counts of the number killed. See: 'NTPC power plant blast: Death toll rises to 32, NHRC serves notice to UP govt'. *Mint.*

Ramana, M.V., 2012. *The power of promise: Examining nuclear energy in India.* Penguin UK.

Kandlikar, M., Somanathan, E., Subramanian, A., 2015. Coal and the climate change debate. Ideas for India.

Chapter 7: Expert Performance

Chowdhury, S., Dey, S., Tripathi, S.N., Beig, G., Mishra, A.K. and Sharma, S., 2017. 'Traffic intervention' policy fails to mitigate air pollution in megacity Delhi. *Environmental Science and Policy*, No. 74, pp. 8–13.

Greenstone, M., Harish, S., Pande, R., and Sudarshan, A., 2017. The Solvable Challenge of Air Pollution in India. *India Policy Forum.*

Ghanem, D. and Zhang, J., 2014. 'Effortless Perfection:' Do Chinese cities manipulate air pollution data?, *Journal of Environmental Economics and Management*, Vol. *68*, No. 2, pp. 203–225.

p. 198: born in health facilities. Coffey, D. and Spears, D. Neonatal death in India: The effect of birth order in a context of maternal undernutrition. Also Coffey, D. The association between neonatal death and facility birth in regions of India. Both 2018 UT Austin working papers.

p. 199: count of deaths. Cohen, *et al.* (2017) estimate over a million annual deaths in India from ambient air pollution, which does not take into consideration household air pollution, which has been estimated to be another half million.

On the Vietnam war:

>   Hirschman, C., Preston, S. and Loi, V.M., 1995. Vietnamese casualties during the American war: A new estimate. *Population and Development Review.*

>   Obermeyer, Z., Murray, C.J. and Gakidou, E., 2008. Fifty years of violent war deaths from Vietnam to Bosnia: analysis of data from the world health survey programme. *BMJ*, Vol. 336, No. 7659, pp. 1482–1486.

On deaths from Indian air pollution:

>   Apte, J.S., Marshall, J.D., Cohen, A.J. and Brauer, M., 2015. Addressing global mortality from ambient $PM_{2.5}$. *Environmental Science & Technology*, Vol., 49, No. 13, pp. 8057–8066.

>   Balakrishnan, K., Cohen, A. and Smith, K.R., 2014. Addressing the burden of disease attributable to air pollution in India: the need to integrate across household and ambient air pollution exposures. *Environmental health perspectives*, Vol. 122, No. 1, p. A6.

>   Cohen, A.J., Brauer, M., Burnett, R., Anderson, H.R., Frostad, J., Estep, K., Balakrishnan, K., Brunekreef, B., Dandona, L., Dandona, R. and Feigin, V., 2017. Estimates and 25-year trends of the global burden of disease attributable to ambient air pollution: an analysis of data from the Global Burden of Diseases Study 2015. *The Lancet*, Vol. 389, No. 10082, pp. 1907–1918.

>   For more references, see the Lancet Commission cited in Chapter 1.

Arendt, H., 1972. *Crises of the republic: Lying in politics, civil disobedience on violence, thoughts on politics, and revolution.* Houghton Mifflin Harcourt. ('Lying in Politics' first appeared in the *New York Review of Books* in 1971.)

Cialdini, R.B., Reno, R.R. and Kallgren, C.A., 1990. A focus theory of normative conduct: recycling the concept of norms to reduce littering in public places. *Journal of Personality and Social Psychology*, Vol. 58, No 6, p. 1015.

Duflo, E., Greenstone, M., Pande, R. and Ryan, N., 2013. Truth-telling by third-party auditors and the response of polluting firms: Experimental evidence from India. The *Quarterly Journal of Economics*, Vol. 128, No. 4, pp. 1499–1545.

p. 204: two similar experiments.

Duflo, E., Hanna, R. and Ryan, S.P., 2012. Incentives work: Getting teachers to come to school. *American Economic Review*, Vol. 102, No. 4, pp. 1241–78.

Banerjee, A.V., Duflo, E. and Glennerster, R., 2008. Putting a Band-Aid on a corpse: Incentives for nurses in the Indian public health care system. *Journal of the European Economic Association*, Vol. 6, No. 2-3, pp. 487–500.

Dubash, N.K. and Joseph, N.B., 2016. Evolution of institutions for climate policy in India. *Economic & Political Weekly*, Vol. 51, No. 3, p. 45.

Kumar, N. and Foster, A.D., 2007. Have CNG regulations in Delhi done their job?. *Economic and Political Weekly*, pp. 48–58. Also see chapter 1 of: Narain, S., 2017. *Conflicts of Interest: My Journey through India's Green Movement*. Penguin. Kathuria, V., 2005. Impact of CNG on Delhi's Air Pollution. *Economic and Political Weekly*, Vol. 40, No. 18.

Tetlock, P.E., 2005. *Expert Political Judgement: How Good Is It? How Can We Know?*. Princeton University Press.

p. 208: overstated success. Hathi, P. and Srivastav, N. 2018. Why we still need to measure open defecation in rural India. *Ideas for India*. 1 October.

Chapter 8: Conclusion

2016. Fire breaks out in Indira Bhawan. The *Times of India*. 20 March.

p. 218: standards keep improving. Harvey, H. 2018. *Designing Climate Solutions: A Policy Guide for Low-Carbon Energy.* Island Press. also: Shapiro, J.S. and Walker, R., 2018. Why is Pollution from US Manufacturing Declining? The Roles of Environmental Regulation, Productivity, and Trade. NBER working paper.

Kahn, M.E. and Zheng, S., 2016. *Blue Skies Over Beijing: Economic Growth and the Environment in China.* Princeton University Press.

Qin, Y., Wagner, F., Scovronick, N., Peng, W., Yang, J., Zhu, T., Smith, K.R. and Mauzerall, D.L., 2017. Air quality, health, and climate implications of China's synthetic natural gas development. *Proceedings of the National Academy of Sciences*, p.201703167.

Freese, B., 2016. *Coal: A Human History.* Basic Books.

Rosling, H., Rönnlund, A.R. and Rosling, O., 2018. *Factfulness: Ten Reasons We're Wrong about the World – And Why Things are Better Than You Think.* Flatiron Books. Also: Pinker, S., 2018. *Enlightenment Now: The case for Reason, Science, Humanism, and Progress.* Penguin.

Arrhenius, G., 2005. The boundary problem in democratic theory. *Democracy Unbound: Basic Explorations I*, pp. 14–29.

Brighouse, H. and Fleurbaey, M., 2010. Democracy and proportionality. *Journal of Political Philosophy*, Vol. 18, No. 2, pp. 137–155.

Achen, C.H. and Bartels, L.M., 2017. *Democracy for Realists: Why Elections do not Produce Responsive Government.* Princeton University Press.

Przeworski, A., 2018. *Why Bother with Elections?*, John Wiley & Sons.

Fujiwara, T., Meng, K. and Vogl, T., 2016. Habit formation in voting: Evidence from rainy elections. *American Economic Journal: Applied Economics*, Vol. 8, No. 4, pp. 160–88.

p. 228: Silicon Valley gift. Cowan, J. 2018. California Today: Silicon Valley's Hot Holiday Gift. *The New York Times*. 5 December.

p. 228: NREGA. Thanks to Yamini Aiyar of CPR for this observation, at a meeting about sanitation policy. See also: Drèze, J., 2002. On research and action. *Economic and Political Weekly*, pp.817–819.

p. 230: citizen activism. See the Environmental Justice Atlas at ejatlas.org.

Chandrasekhar, A. 2018. Jharkhand villagers ask why should they lose land for Adani project supplying power to Bangladesh. scroll.in. 13 June.

Amnesty International India. 2016. 'When land is lost, do we eat coal?': Coal mining and violations of Adivasi rights in India.

2018. CM Yogi to lay foundation of 660 MP plant at Panki. The *Times of India*. 1 January.

p. 232: Environmental Impact Assessment. Environmental Impact Assessment Study Report for Proposed Expansion 1x660 MW Panki Coal Based Supercritical Thermal Power Project, District: Kanpur (U.P.). It explains: 'Terms of Reference (TOR) for the 1X660 MW Panki Extension was granted by Ministry of Environment & Forest (MOEF) vide letter no-J-13012/35/2013-IA.I(T) Dated 16.09.2014 is enclosed as Annexure 1.'

Reid, David. 2017. Inside India's humongous solar plant. *BBC*. 20 June.

Acknowledgements

This book is made of co-authored research. I could not have done much of it without my friends and collaborators from whom I have learned much. At r.i.c.e., I have been grateful to work with Aashish Gupta, Nikhil Srivastav, and Sangita Vyas on air pollution; Diane Coffey, Payal Hathi, Nidhi Khurana, and Amit Thorat on the SARI survey; Avinash Kishore when he planted this seed; and Nazar Khalid and the whole r.i.c.e team on the 2018 rural survey. Nikhil Srivastav was indispensable in qualitative field research.

Everyone at Princeton University's Climate Futures Initiative has taught me: thanks especially to Marc Fleurbaey for welcoming me on to the team, and to Mark Budolfson and Noah Scovronick for long hours collaborating over Skype. At Texas, Josh Apte, Mike Geruso, Kevin Kuruc, and Melissa LoPalo; Sagnik Dey and Sourangsu Chowdhury at IIT Delhi; Navroz Dubash at CPR.

I appreciate feedback on drafts from Drew Burd, Subha Ganguly, Neeta Goel, Vasudha Jain, Avani Kapur, Kevin Kuruc, Melissa LoPalo, Unnati Mehta, and Noah Scovronick. Along the way I met with or otherwise learned from Gustaf

Arrhenius, Alan Barreca, John Broome, Krister Bykvist, Shoibal Chakravarty, Tom Clasen, Prodipto Ghosh, Sarath Guttikunda, Jeff Hammer, Kelsey Jack, Grant Miller, Paulina Oliva, Kirk Smith, and Sachchida Nand Tripathi. At HarperCollins India, Udayan Mitra and especially Arcopol Chaudhuri and Prema Govindan, who helped me turn this into the book you are reading. During one of the months of writing, I enjoyed a visit to the Institute for Futures Studies in Stockholm.

Mark Budolfson (who never wavered in his enthusiasm for this book), Diane Coffey, Aashish Gupta, and Sanigta Vyas gave detailed and thoughtful comments that improved the whole book. I am lucky that these four – plus Navroz Dubash (who may or may not have successfully kept me from writing the wrong book), Mike Geruso (for talking about it just the right amount), and Nikhil Srivastav (for everything) – have left fingerprints throughout the book. Thank you, all.